TOM BRADY BIOGRAPHY: THE RELENTLESS PURSUIT OF GREATNESS

From Unwanted Draft Pick to the Greatest of All Time

Bobby M. Kim

TOM BRADY BIOGRAPHY:

All Rights Reserved, No part of this publication may be reproduced, distributed room transmitted in any form or by any means, including photocopying, recording, or other electronic or mechanical methods without the prior written permission of the publisher except in the case of brief quotations embodied in critical reviews and certain other non-commercial uses permitted by copyright law.

Copyright ©2025

By Bobby M. Kim

TOM BRADY BIOGRAPHY:

TABLE OF CONTENTS

INTRODUCTION
CHAPTER ONE: GROWING UP IN SAN MATEO:
CHAPTER TWO: The MICHIGAN YEARS – FIGHTING FOR A CHANCE
CHAPTER THREE: THE 2000 NFL DRAFT – THE ULTIMATE SNUB
CHAPTER FOUR: STEPPING IN, STEPPING UP
CHAPTER FIVE: PROVING IT WASN'T A FLUKE – BUILDING A DYNASTY
CHAPTER SIX: THE PERFECT SEASON THAT WASN'T – 2007 AND THE 18-1 HEARTBREAK
CHAPTER SEVEN: THE INJURY of 2008: A CAREER IN PERIL THE MOMENT THAT CHANGED EVERYTHING
CHAPTER EIGHT: A HISTORIC PARTNERSHIP IN THE BRADY-BELICHICK ERA
CHAPTER NINE: THE GREATEST SUPER BOWL EVER: THE 28-3 COMEBACK
CHAPTER TEN: LESSONS FROM TOM BRADY – WHAT WE CAN LEARN FROM HIS JOURNEY
CONCLUSION

TOM BRADY BIOGRAPHY:

INTRODUCTION

The Development of a Legend Sports has stories that captivate, motivate, and shape generations. Then, there is the story of Tom Brady—a tale so improbable, so relentless, and so unparalleled that it has transcended football itself. In addition to being a tale of athletic dominance, his journey is a masterclass in perseverance, self-confidence, and an unwavering obsession with greatness. Brady wasn't born into stardom. He was not predicted to become the next big thing. There were no predetermined routes to success, no guarantees, and no shortcuts. He was overlooked, doubted, and nearly forgotten. He went from an afterthought in the 2000 NFL Draft to the greatest quarterback in NFL history—a seven-time Super Bowl champion, a five-time Super Bowl MVP, and the undisputed architect of a football dynasty—through sheer willpower, meticulous preparation, and an obsession with improvement. His career was not defined by one moment, one season, or even one decade—it was a two-decade-long reign of dominance, spanning multiple eras, rule changes, and generational shifts. Brady redefined what it meant to be a quarterback, what it meant to be a leader, and, ultimately, what it meant to be the greatest of all time.

This is more than just a Tom Brady biography. It is an exploration of what separates good from great, great from legendary, and legendary from immortal. It provides an in-depth look at the mindset, preparation, and sacrifices that enabled Brady to defy critics, the laws of athletic decline, and even his own age. Whether you are a football fan, an athlete, or simply someone looking for inspiration, Brady's journey offers invaluable lessons on work ethic, resilience, and the relentless pursuit of excellence.

Why Tom Brady's Story Is Important Every sport has its icons—Michael Jordan in basketball, Muhammad Ali in boxing, Serena Williams in tennis, and Wayne Gretzky in hockey. These athletes didn't just dominate their respective fields; they redefined them. Tom Brady belongs in this conversation, not just because of his rings, but because of the way he changed the very fabric of the NFL.

Before Brady, quarterbacks were often considered past their prime in their late 30s. He played until he was 45. A sixth-round draft pick was never expected to save a team before Brady. He became the league's face.

TOM BRADY BIOGRAPHY:

Before Brady, the idea of winning seven Super Bowls seemed unfathomable. He did it, spanning two different teams and two different eras.

But what makes Brady's journey even more fascinating is the adversity he overcame to get there. He wasn't the fastest. He wasn't the most powerful. He wasn't the most naturally gifted. What he had was something more valuable—an insatiable hunger to be better, an obsessive attention to detail, and a fire that burned hotter every time he was doubted.

The story of Brady isn't just for football fans. It's for anyone who has ever been told they weren't good enough. It's for the underdogs, the overlooked, and those willing to put in the work when no one is watching. It's about proving that talent alone doesn't determine success—relentless effort does.

The Relentless Pursuit of Greatness

If there's one word that defines Brady's career, it's relentless. He was relentless in his preparation, relentless in his self-discipline, and relentless in his pursuit of perfection.

Not only was his training regimen legendary for its endurance but also for its intensity. While others saw decline, Brady sought improvement. He studied film obsessively, treating every game like a puzzle to be solved. He developed the TB12 Method, an approach to fitness and nutrition that allowed him to outlast quarterbacks half his age.

But more than his preparation, it was his mental edge that set him apart. Over the course of more than two decades, Brady acted as though he were still the slender Michigan kid who was left out of the draft. He thrived under pressure, embraced adversity, and treated every moment—whether a preseason game or the Super Bowl—as an opportunity to prove himself.

The mindset and preparation that made Brady great will be the subject of this book, which will also go beyond the records and stats. It will dive into the moments that defined him, the relationships that shaped him, and the rivalries that fueled him. From the infamous "Tuck Rule" game to the shocking Deflategate scandal, from the heartbreak of Super Bowl losses to the unparalleled triumphs of seven championships, this is the full story of how Tom Brady became the greatest quarterback of all time.

From 199th Pick to the GOAT

TOM BRADY BIOGRAPHY:

The NFL Draft of 2000, when six quarterbacks were selected ahead of Tom Brady, may be the most enduring sporting event of all time. Every year, footage resurfaces of Brady's combine workout, a now-iconic video of an unremarkable-looking quarterback with a sluggish 40-yard dash and unimpressive measurables. Scouts were unimpressed. He was dismissed by analysts. Even the Patriots, the team that would go on to draft him, saw him as nothing more than a backup project.

He did, however, win his first Super Bowl trophy in just two seasons. Within a decade, he had built the most dominant dynasty in football history. And by the time he walked away from the game at age 45, he had shattered every expectation, every record, and every doubt ever cast upon him.

His life is one of perseverance, faith, and persistent self-improvement. It's about what happens when preparation meets opportunity. It's about turning doubt into fuel and adversity into advantage.

The Road Ahead

This book will take you on the journey of Tom Brady's life—from his childhood in San Mateo, California, to his early struggles at Michigan, to his legendary run in New England, and finally, his unexpected but triumphant second act in Tampa Bay. It will explore the highs, the lows, the controversies, the championships, and the sacrifices that made him the most decorated player in football history.

Whether you watched Brady dominate for two decades or are just now discovering the legend of TB12, this book will give you a deeper understanding of the man behind the records, the mindset behind the success, and the relentless pursuit that turned a sixth-round pick into the greatest of all time.

His journey wasn't about proving others wrong—it was about proving himself right.

And in doing so, he changed the game forever.

TOM BRADY BIOGRAPHY:

CHAPTER ONE: GROWING UP IN SAN MATEO:

Humble Roots A childhood centered on family in the heart of California Tom Brady was born on August 3, 1977, in San Mateo, California, a city in the San Francisco Bay Area. With his parents, Tom Brady Sr. and Galynn Patricia Brady, and his three older sisters, Maureen, Julie, and Nancy, he was raised in a close-knit, middle-class household. The youngest and only boy in a household of competitive siblings, Brady's childhood was shaped by the energy and drive of his family.

The values of discipline, respect, and perseverance were instilled in him by his hardworking parents. Galynn Brady managed the household while his father, Tom Brady Sr., worked in insurance. They both emphasized the value of effort and commitment, ensuring their children pursue their passions wholeheartedly.

Growing up with three older sisters meant Tom was constantly challenged athletically. Each of his sisters was accomplished in sports—Maureen was a star softball pitcher who earned a college scholarship, and Julie and Nancy also excelled in athletics. Watching his sisters succeed made young Tom naturally competitive, pushing him to work harder in sports even when he was not the most physically gifted player on the field.

San Mateo, located just south of San Francisco, was a lively, suburban environment that gave Brady access to a strong community and plenty of opportunities to play sports. The culture of the Bay Area, especially in the 1980s, was rich with sports influence. The region was home to the San Francisco 49ers, who were in the midst of their dynasty, with Joe Montana and Jerry Rice dominating the NFL. As a child, Brady was deeply inspired by Montana, idolizing him and dreaming of one day following in his footsteps.

Formative Years: The Power of Early Influence

Brady's early interest in football is largely attributable to his family's dedication to the sport. Tom's father, a fervent supporter of the 49ers, frequently took him to Candlestick Park to watch games. Some of Brady's fondest childhood memories involve sitting in the stands, watching Montana orchestrate game-winning drives. The young boy's mind was sown with ambition by the excitement of those times. At home, Brady would often

TOM BRADY BIOGRAPHY:

reenact Montana's legendary plays in his backyard. He would throw passes to fictitious receivers, imitating his idol's poise and precision. His enthusiasm for the sport grew as a result of this early connection, as did his keen awareness of football. Though football would eventually become his claim to fame, Brady's childhood was not solely dedicated to the sport. He played baseball and basketball as well, demonstrating his versatility as an athlete. In fact, many believed his best sport was baseball—he was a talented left-handed hitter and a capable catcher. He even had the potential to play Major League Baseball, according to scouts. Despite this, Brady's heart belonged to football. He adored the challenge of leading a team, the game's intensity, and the involved strategy. Football, in contrast to baseball, where individual performance is frequently isolated, required a strong bond between teammates. As a natural leader, Brady gravitated toward the quarterback position, even though he was far from the most physically gifted player on the field.

Organized Football's Slow Start Despite his passion for the game, Brady was not a highly sought-after young athlete. Unlike many future NFL quarterbacks who dominate their youth leagues, Brady was often overlooked in his early football days. During his childhood, he did not stand out as an exceptional player. Brady played as both a backup quarterback and a quarterback when he first joined the Pop Warner football league in his area. He wasn't particularly fast, didn't have the strongest arm, and lacked the physical size that many elite young quarterbacks display. In fact, his coaches often doubted whether he had the ability to succeed at the position.

This could have discouraged him, but Brady was resilient. His father, always supportive, helped him stay motivated, often reminding him that hard work and persistence were more important than natural talent. His mother, too, played a crucial role in keeping him grounded, ensuring he never let disappointments keep him from improving.

Brady's early struggles in football were an important part of his journey. They reinforced a lesson that would define his career: success is not given; it is earned through relentless effort. Brady's mentality of fighting for every opportunity endured throughout his life, in contrast to that of many elite

TOM BRADY BIOGRAPHY:

athletes who dominate from a young age. High School Years: The Making of a Quarterback

Brady attended Junípero Serra High School, a private Catholic school in San Mateo. At first, he didn't stand out as an athlete. He was the junior varsity team's backup quarterback as a freshman, so he watched most of the games from the sidelines. He was not the biggest, fastest, or strongest player on the team. Other quarterbacks had quicker feet and stronger arms. However, Brady had something that set him apart—his work ethic and mental toughness. While others relied on their physical gifts, Brady focused on studying the game, understanding defensive schemes, and mastering the small details that made quarterbacks great.

He spent extra hours watching game film, analyzing his mistakes, and working on his footwork. He had an almost obsessive dedication to improvement, constantly asking his coaches for advice and implementing their feedback. His leadership skills also began to develop during this time. Even as an underclassman, he showed a natural ability to rally his teammates and keep them motivated.

By his junior year, Brady finally earned the starting quarterback position. Though he still wasn't a highly recruited athlete, his ability to lead and manage the game started turning heads. He did a good job on the field, but nothing extraordinary. Although his numbers weren't particularly impressive, it was already clear that he was capable of making decisions and remaining composed under pressure. During his senior year, he began attracting more attention. His confidence increased as his throwing mechanics improved. Though still not a top-tier prospect, he started receiving interest from college programs. However, numerous recruiters remained unsure whether he possessed the necessary physical attributes for advancement. Brady faced a pivotal moment in his senior year when he had to decide between pursuing football or baseball. He was drafted by the Montreal Expos in the 18th round of the 1995 Major League Baseball Draft. The Expos saw potential in him as a catcher, believing he had the intelligence and hand-eye coordination to excel in the MLB.

Brady chose football over professional baseball despite the possibility. Even though others doubted him, he believed that he could improve as a

TOM BRADY BIOGRAPHY:

quarterback. This decision reflected his unwavering confidence in himself—a trait that would later define his NFL career.

Lessons from San Mateo: The Foundations of Greatness

The years Brady spent growing up in San Mateo shaped him into an athlete and a person. His childhood was not defined by early stardom or instant success. Instead, it was characterized by tenacity, hard work, and unwavering confidence in himself. Every experience shaped his tenacious mentality, from his time as a backup quarterback in high school to his idolization of Joe Montana at Candlestick Park. His family, especially his sisters and parents, provided the foundation for his work ethic and competitiveness.

San Mateo was not just where he grew up; it was where he learned how to overcome obstacles, how to ignore doubters, and how to bet on himself when no one else would. These lessons would carry him through college at Michigan and into the NFL, where he would defy expectations at every turn. Brady's early years were not about immediate greatness. They were about resilience, persistence, and laying the groundwork for one of the most legendary careers in sports history.

Family's influence: a supportive but competitive environment Tom Brady's family's strong sense of unity and competitiveness had a big impact on his upbringing in San Mateo. As the youngest of four siblings, Brady was surrounded by three older sisters—Maureen, Julie, and Nancy—who were not only athletically gifted but also fiercely competitive. His mentality and work ethic were significantly influenced by this dynamic. His eldest sister, Maureen, was a standout softball pitcher who earned a scholarship to Fresno State, becoming an All-American. Julie and Nancy also excelled in sports, pushing themselves to achieve success in whatever they pursued. Brady was constantly in an environment where effort and determination were non-negotiable with such accomplished siblings. While some younger siblings might have been discouraged by the pressure of living up to their older siblings' success, Brady embraced it. He looked up to his sisters as role models because of how dedicated they were to training and how resilient they were when faced with difficulties. The idea that perseverance and consistent effort were the keys to success was reinforced in this family setting. His competitive nature was particularly influenced by his father,

TOM BRADY BIOGRAPHY:

Tom Brady Sr. Brady Sr., an avid sports fan, took young Tom to numerous sporting events, particularly Candlestick Park games for the San Francisco 49ers. He also encouraged competitions in the backyard, challenging Tom to various sports-related tasks, which helped Tom become even more competitive. His mother, Galynn, provided balance by instilling humility and emotional strength in her son. She was a calming presence in his life, ensuring that while he pursued his athletic dreams, he remained grounded and respectful. She taught him to accept defeat with grace and never to give up, even when he won. Brady had a unique perspective because he was constantly motivated to improve while always having the emotional stability provided by his parents and siblings. This combination of intense competition and unwavering family support gave Brady that perspective. It was a foundation that would serve him well throughout his career, especially when facing adversity.

Joe Montana: The Childhood Hero Who Became a Blueprint for Success

Brady was fortunate to witness one of the greatest football dynasties—the San Francisco 49ers under Joe Montana—while he was growing up in the Bay Area in the 1980s. Known for his cool demeanor, clutch performances, and surgical precision as a passer, Montana won four Super Bowls. Young Tom Brady idolized him, watching every game and memorizing his every move. Brady enjoyed the atmosphere at Candlestick Park when his father took him to games and dreamed of one day playing in the NFL. One of the most defining moments of his childhood came during the 1981 NFC Championship Game, when Montana orchestrated "The Catch" – a legendary touchdown pass to Dwight Clark in the closing moments against the Dallas Cowboys. That moment solidified Montana's greatness in Brady's eyes and became a source of inspiration for him.

Brady wasn't just a fan; he studied Montana. He looked at how well he could walk, make decisions, and keep his cool under pressure. While most kids his age were simply watching football for entertainment, Brady was mentally dissecting the game, absorbing the nuances of quarterback play.

Montana's influence on Brady extended beyond just the mechanics of football. He admired Montana's leadership, modesty, and capacity to triumph without pursuing personal glory. These qualities would later become hallmarks of Brady's own career, as he embodied a team-first

TOM BRADY BIOGRAPHY:

mentality throughout his time in the NFL. Brady's aspirations to play football were significantly influenced by his childhood fascination with Montana. It wasn't just about wanting to play in the NFL—it was about wanting to play quarterback at the highest level and win championships like his idol.

Early Struggles: Overcoming the Odds in Youth Football

The beginnings of Brady's involvement in organized football were far from glamorous. Brady struggled to stand out from many other future NFL quarterbacks who dominate their youth leagues. When he first joined the local Pop Warner football league as a young boy, he was far from the most physically gifted player. He lacked speed, arm strength, and the natural athleticism that many of his peers possessed. At times, he wasn't even the first-choice quarterback on his own youth team.

However, he made up for his lack of raw talent with determination. Brady demonstrated a willingness to work harder than anyone else from a young age. He honed his accuracy by throwing footballs through tire swings for hours in his backyard. He examined the throwing motions and decision-making processes of other great quarterbacks as well as Montana in game footage. One defining moment in his youth football career came when he was initially placed as a backup quarterback. It's possible that many young players in his position would have accepted that position or even thought about switching positions. Brady, on the other hand, refused to give up. He treated every practice like a game, putting in extra hours to prove himself to his coaches and teammates.

His persistence eventually paid off, as he gradually earned more playing time. Though he was never the biggest or fastest player on the field, he demonstrated intelligence, leadership, and an ability to stay composed under pressure—traits that would later define his NFL career.

Multi-Sport Athlete: How Baseball Nearly Changed His Path

While football was his passion, Brady was also an exceptional baseball player. At Junípero Serra High School, he played catcher and had a powerful left-handed swing. In fact, professional baseball scouts were impressed by his talent. In the 1995 MLB Draft, the Montreal Expos selected Brady in the 18th round, believing he had the potential to develop into a major league player. The Expos saw him as a future star catcher due to his strong arm and leadership skills behind the plate.

TOM BRADY BIOGRAPHY:

Brady had a difficult decision to make—pursue a career in baseball, where he had a clear path to the professional ranks, or take the riskier route of playing college football, where he was far from a guaranteed success.

Despite the allure of professional baseball, Brady chose football. It was a decision driven by passion rather than security. Even though many people doubted him, he believed he could become a great quarterback. He was aware that he had more to prove in football. This choice reflected the essence of Brady's mentality—he was never one to take the easy road. He embraced challenges, knowing that true greatness comes from overcoming adversity.

The Influence of Junípero Serra High School

Brady's time at Junípero Serra High School was pivotal in shaping his football career. The school, known for producing athletes like Barry Bonds and Lynn Swann, had a strong sports culture. However, when Brady arrived as a freshman, he was far from an immediate standout.

As a sophomore, he played on the junior varsity team and didn't see much action. In comparison to athletes with greater natural talent, he was an afterthought. But instead of getting discouraged, Brady focused on improving.

His turning point came when he dedicated himself to intense offseason training. He worked tirelessly to improve his throwing mechanics, studying the game with an almost obsessive dedication. He spent countless hours working with coaches, analyzing film, and refining his footwork.

By his junior year, he earned the starting quarterback position, and though he wasn't a dominant player, he showed flashes of his potential. He led his team with poise and intelligence, making smart decisions and demonstrating a remarkable ability to remain calm under pressure.

During his senior season, he began attracting attention from college recruiters, though he was far from a five-star prospect. He was an unheralded quarterback with potential but not the physical tools that typically draw major offers.

Despite this, Brady believed in himself. He sent out highlight tapes to various college programs, hoping to earn a scholarship. Eventually, the University of Michigan took a chance on him, offering him a spot on their roster. This marked the next chapter of Brady's journey—a journey that

TOM BRADY BIOGRAPHY:

would continue to be defined by resilience, self-belief, and a relentless pursuit of greatness.

TOM BRADY BIOGRAPHY:

CHAPTER TWO: The MICHIGAN YEARS – FIGHTING FOR A CHANCE

The Michigan Years – Fighting for a Chance
 An Unheralded Recruit at Michigan: A Tough Beginning Tom Brady made a life-altering decision to attend the prestigious and long-standing football program at the University of Michigan in 1995. Michigan was a powerhouse in college football, known for producing elite quarterbacks and competing at the highest level in the Big Ten Conference. For a young quarterback looking to prove himself, it was both an opportunity and a daunting challenge.
 Despite being a talented high school player, Brady was not a highly sought-after recruit. He was only a three-star prospect, and many colleges didn't even look at him. He did well in high school, but unlike Peyton Manning, who was the best quarterback recruit in his class, he was not regarded as a top talent. Michigan took a chance on him, but when he arrived on campus in Ann Arbor, he quickly realized how far he was from being a starting quarterback. The Wolverines were already stacked at the position, with experienced upperclassmen ahead of him on the depth chart. Power running and conservative passing were the foundations of Michigan's offense at the time, and quarterbacks needed to be both physically strong and highly intelligent to succeed. Brady's first experience in a Michigan uniform was humbling. He was buried on the depth chart as the seventh-string quarterback, meaning there were six players ahead of him. It was a crushing reality check for a young player who had dreamed of becoming Joe Montana. He wasn't just fighting for playing time—he was fighting for relevance.
 Struggling with Self-Doubt: The Psychological Battle
 There was a lot of self-doubt, frustration, and internal struggle during Brady's early Michigan years. As a freshman, he barely saw any reps in practice, often spending entire sessions watching from the sidelines. On the roster, he wasn't the strongest, fastest, or most physically imposing quarterback. Brady felt invisible because the coaching staff focused on the upperclassmen. There were moments when he questioned whether he had made the right choice by coming to Michigan. At one point, he even

TOM BRADY BIOGRAPHY:

considered transferring to a smaller school where he might have a better chance to play. The idea of leaving Michigan crossed his mind multiple times, but each time, he decided to stay and fight.

One of the key figures who helped Brady through this difficult period was Greg Harden, Michigan's sports psychologist. Harden had worked with many athletes struggling with confidence and mental resilience. He poured out his frustrations during Brady's meeting with him, saying that he felt overlooked, that he wasn't sure if he was good enough, and that he didn't see a path to playing time. Harden gave Brady advice that would change his mindset forever. He advised him that taking full control of his attitude and preparation was the only way to dispel his doubts. He needed to concentrate on getting better each day rather than worrying about what other people thought, treating each practice like the biggest game of his life. Brady took this advice to heart. He started waking up at 5 AM to lift weights, staying after practice to throw extra passes, and studying film obsessively. He understood that if he couldn't control how much playing time he got, he could at least control how hard he worked.

The Weight Room and Film Study: Building a Quarterback's Mindset

If there was one thing Brady lacked when he arrived at Michigan, it was physical development. He was tall at 6'4", but he was thin, weighing only about 195 pounds. Compared to other quarterbacks who had filled out their frames through years of intense training, Brady looked underdeveloped.

Although Brady didn't immediately stand out, Michigan's strength and conditioning program was one of the best in the country. His speed and agility were below average, and his arm strength, while decent, wasn't considered elite. He had to work twice as hard just to keep up.

Brady committed himself to transforming his body. He spent extra hours in the weight room, working on building strength and endurance. He was put on a strict diet and exercise plan by the coaching staff to help him build muscle and become more athletic. He gradually increased his weight to around 215 pounds, adding the muscle necessary to withstand hits from Big Ten defenders.

But what really separated Brady was his film study. While other players relied on their athletic gifts, Brady realized that intelligence could be his

TOM BRADY BIOGRAPHY:

greatest weapon. He studied film obsessively, breaking down defenses and learning the nuances of Michigan's offensive system.
 He spent countless hours deciphering how opponents concealed their coverages, and he developed a fascination with defensive strategies. He started anticipating plays before they happened, understanding where defenders would be before the ball was even snapped. This level of preparation would later become his trademark in the NFL, but it all started at Michigan.
 Battling for Playing Time: The Long Road to Becoming QB1
 Brady redshirted his freshman year in 1995, meaning he didn't play in any games. Instead, he spent the year practicing with the scout team, running plays against Michigan's starting defense. While it was a frustrating experience at times, it helped him improve his timing and decision-making under pressure.
 By his sophomore year in 1996, Brady had moved up the depth chart, but he was still far from being the starter. Brian Griese, a talented and experienced quarterback, was firmly entrenched as Michigan's leader. Griese would eventually lead Michigan to a national championship in 1997, making it nearly impossible for Brady to see meaningful playing time.
 Despite being stuck as a backup, Brady refused to become complacent. He treated every practice like a competition, pushing himself to improve even when he knew he wouldn't start.
 One of his biggest strengths was his ability to learn from others. He closely observed Griese, studying how he prepared for games, how he handled pressure, and how he commanded the huddle. He took mental notes on everything, filing away lessons that he would apply when his own time came.
 The Turning Point: Junior Year and the Quarterback Controversy
 By 1998, Brady was a junior, and for the first time, he had a legitimate chance to compete for the starting job. Griese had left the team, leaving a quarterback vacancy. However, the competition was fierce. Michigan had just recruited Drew Henson, a highly touted freshman who was considered one of the best quarterback prospects in the country. Henson was everything Brady wasn't—physically gifted, strong-armed, and an elite athlete. Many believed he would take over as Michigan's starter

TOM BRADY BIOGRAPHY:

immediately. The coaching staff was enamored with Henson's potential, and Brady once again found himself in a battle for playing time.

However, something had changed in Brady. He was no longer the shy, self-doubting freshman who questioned whether he belonged at Michigan. He had spent three years sharpening his skills, improving his mechanics, and developing a deep understanding of the game. He was ready to prove himself. Brady outworked everyone in training camp. He was the first to arrive at practice and the last to leave. He put in more effort than ever before, refusing to let another quarterback seize his chance. Michigan's head coach, Lloyd Carr, was initially hesitant about naming Brady the starter. He saw the potential in Henson and wanted to give him opportunities. But Brady's leadership and performance in practice made it impossible to ignore him.

When the 1998 season began, Carr named Brady the starting quarterback, though he continued to rotate Henson into games. This led to a frustrating situation where Brady had to constantly prove himself, even after winning games.

Despite the pressure, Brady responded with clutch performances. He led Michigan to a 10-3 record, throwing for 2,636 yards and 15 touchdowns. More importantly, he showed an ability to lead late-game comebacks, something that would define his NFL career.

The Captain vs. Quarterback Debate in Senior Year As the 1999 season approached, Tom Brady faced yet another uphill battle. Despite proving himself as a capable starter in his junior year, he still wasn't guaranteed the job outright. The shadow of Drew Henson loomed larger than ever. Henson, Michigan's prized recruit, was seen as the future of the program. He had the kind of raw talent that made NFL scouts swoon, mobility, and an elite arm. Many Michigan fans and even some within the coaching staff believed Henson should be given the starting role immediately. However, Brady refused to step aside. He had spent four years battling for every opportunity, and he wasn't going to let anyone take his job without a fight.

Brady put in a lot of effort during the offseason to get ready for his senior year. He put in a lot of time in the weight room, which helped him build more muscle. He refined his mechanics, working on his footwork and quickening his release. But most importantly, he improved his mental

TOM BRADY BIOGRAPHY:

performance. His leadership had also become undeniable. He was named team captain, a title that meant everything to him. It was proof that his teammates respected him—not because of his natural talent, but because of his work ethic, perseverance, and ability to lead under pressure.

Still, Michigan head coach Lloyd Carr wasn't fully convinced. Carr announced that Michigan would use a quarterback rotation, splitting playing time between Brady and Henson. It was a frustrating situation for Brady, who had already spent years proving himself, only to be told that he would have to share the position once again.

Proving Himself on the Field: The Defining Games of Brady's College Career

Despite the quarterback controversy, Brady remained unfazed. He was determined to let his play do the talking, and as the season unfolded, he delivered some of the most clutch performances of his career.

"The Drive": Penn State's comeback victory Brady's college career came to a head on November 13, 1999, during a game against Penn State. Michigan was trailing 27-17 in the fourth quarter, and with time running out, the Wolverines needed a miracle. Brady took control of the offense with absolute composure. He led Michigan on a game-winning 89-yard drive, throwing precision passes and managing the clock perfectly. He gave tight end Shawn Thompson a touchdown pass to end the drive, securing the dramatic 31-27 victory. It was the kind of performance that showcased everything Brady had become known for—poise under pressure, precise decision-making, and an unshakable belief in himself. Even though Henson continued to get playing time, Brady had clearly proven that he was the team's leader when the game was on the line.

The 1999 Michigan vs. Ohio State Rivalry Game

One of the most intense rivalries in college football is between Michigan and Ohio State. For Brady, the 1999 contest would be one of his biggest games. Michigan needed a win against Ohio State in front of more than 100,000 fans in The Big House to keep their Big Ten title hopes alive. Ohio State had a strong team. Michigan prevailed 24-17 thanks to Brady's clutch performance, in which he threw for 300 yards and four touchdowns. He had demonstrated once more that he was at his best when under pressure. The Orange Bowl: Brady's College Career Ends in Spectacular Fashion

TOM BRADY BIOGRAPHY:

Brady's final game as a Wolverine came in the 2000 Orange Bowl against Alabama. He could use this opportunity to demonstrate his readiness for the next level. The game turned into a shootout, with both teams trading blows. Once again, Michigan found itself trailing in the fourth quarter. And once again, Brady stepped up. He threw for 369 yards and 4 touchdowns, including two in overtime. Michigan ultimately won 35-34 after an Alabama missed extra point, capping off Brady's college career in dramatic fashion.

Even though the game ended in victory, there was no celebration for Brady. As soon as the final whistle blew, he walked straight to the locker room, as if he already knew—his journey was far from over.

The NFL Draft Process: Overlooked and Undervalued

Despite his strong senior season and his clutch performances, Brady still wasn't considered an elite NFL prospect. He lacked the physical attributes that scouts were looking for: he wasn't particularly quick, he didn't have a lot of arm strength, and his build wasn't right for an NFL quarterback.

Things did not improve when he attended the NFL Scouting Combine. His 40-yard dash time was a slow 5.28 seconds, one of the worst among quarterbacks. His physique was unimpressive—when he took off his shirt for the weigh-in, he looked more like a regular college student than a future NFL star.

Scouts saw him as a backup at best, someone who might make an NFL roster but wasn't likely to become a franchise quarterback.

But what they didn't measure was his intelligence, leadership, and drive—the qualities that would eventually make him the greatest quarterback of all time.

Brady was unaware of his draft location. He had interviews with a few teams, but most showed little interest. He sat at home with his family on draft day, waiting for his name to be called, as quarterback after quarterback was selected before him.

The Sixth-Round Pick: A Humbling Moment That Changed His Life

Brady watched as six other quarterbacks were selected before him. Players like Chad Pennington, Tee Martin, and Giovanni Carmazzi were taken while he remained undrafted. The rounds went by—one, two, three, four, five—until finally, in the sixth round, with the 199th overall pick, the New England Patriots selected Tom Brady. It was a time of relief and

TOM BRADY BIOGRAPHY:

disappointment all at once. He had been drafted, but barely. He knew that he wasn't being brought in as a future star—he would be an afterthought on the Patriots' roster, a long shot to even make the team.

But deep inside, Brady knew something that nobody else did—this was just the beginning. He had spent his entire life proving people wrong, and this was just another challenge.

As he packed his bags for New England, he carried with him the same mentality that had defined his Michigan years: He would fight for a chance. And he wouldn't stop until he became the best.

TOM BRADY BIOGRAPHY:

CHAPTER THREE: THE 2000 NFL DRAFT – THE ULTIMATE SNUB

Brady's Draft-Day Experience: The Long Wait Begins Tom Brady woke up on the morning of April 15, 2000, knowing that this would be one of the most important days of his life. He had spent years dreaming of playing in the NFL, but as draft day arrived, he had no guarantees. He was not likely to be taken in the first round. He wasn't even a lock to be drafted at all.

Brady sat at home in San Mateo, California, surrounded by his family. His parents, Tom Sr. and Galynn, were there, along with his three older sisters. A mixture of excitement and nervous energy filled the house. Brady's agent, Don Yee, had prepared him for the reality of the situation. Based on conversations with teams, he informed Brady that he would probably be selected in the middle to late round. There was interest from a few teams, but nothing concrete. Some teams had told Yee that they liked Brady's leadership and intelligence but had concerns about his physical attributes.

Brady, nevertheless, had hope. He had previously been questioned, but he had always found a way to disprove them. He just needed one team to believe in him.

The First Round: The Big Names Go Off the Board

As the draft kicked off, Brady wasn't even watching. He knew there was no chance he'd be selected in the first round. Instead, he went for a run to clear his mind.

Meanwhile, teams were making their selections, and quarterbacks were coming off the board.

The first quarterback taken was Chad Pennington, who went to the New York Jets with the 18th overall pick. Pennington had been a standout at Marshall, and many scouts believed he had the best combination of accuracy, intelligence, and mechanics.

Brady barely paid attention. He knew Pennington was a first-round talent. But as the first day of the draft continued, he started to get nervous.

He had hoped to advance to the third or fourth round at the very least. But as more quarterbacks were selected, he remained on the board.

The Middle Rounds: The Frustration Builds

TOM BRADY BIOGRAPHY:

Brady and his family had been closely following the draft up until the third and fourth rounds. He had spoken with a few teams leading up to the draft, including the San Francisco 49ers, New Orleans Saints, Pittsburgh Steelers, and New England Patriots.

His first team was the 49ers. Growing up, he had idolized Joe Montana and Steve Young, and he had dreamed of wearing the red and gold. But when San Francisco was on the clock in the third round, they passed on him. Instead, they selected Giovanni Carmazzi, a quarterback from Hofstra.

That one stung.

Carmazzi had been highly regarded by some scouts because of his athleticism and strong arm, but he had never played in a major college program. He was seen as a project quarterback, someone who could develop over time.

It was unbelievable to Brady. He had played at Michigan, a powerhouse football program, against elite competition, and yet a quarterback from Hofstra was taken before him?

More quarterbacks followed.

Chris Redman (Louisville) – 75th overall, Baltimore Ravens

Tee Martin (Tennessee) – Pittsburgh Steelers, 163rd overall Marc Bulger (West Virginia) – 168th overall, New Orleans Saints

Texas State's Spergon Wynn, 183rd overall, Cleveland Browns Brady was angry as he watched as six quarterbacks were chosen ahead of him. Some of them had never played in a high-pressure environment like he had at Michigan.

His parents could see the disappointment on his face. At one point, he walked outside to be alone. He didn't want his family to see him upset, but inside, he was hurting.

The call that changed everything in the sixth round Brady was losing hope as the draft dragged into the sixth round. He knew there was a chance he wouldn't be drafted at all.

Then, his phone rang.

A group from Foxborough, Massachusetts, was the one. On the other end of the line was Bill Belichick, the head coach of the New England Patriots.

"Tom, we're about to make you a New England Patriot," Belichick said.

TOM BRADY BIOGRAPHY:

Brady felt a wave of relief wash over him. He didn't care that it was the sixth round. He didn't care that 198 players had been selected before him. He was selected in the end. Tom Brady was selected by the Patriots with the 199th overall pick. The aftermath: mixed feelings The moment was bittersweet. His family cheered, hugging him and celebrating. However, there was no big celebration. Brady knew what being a sixth-round pick meant—he wasn't guaranteed anything.

Sixth-round picks frequently did not make the team, in contrast to first-round quarterbacks, who were anticipated to start and be the face of a franchise. He would be a longshot to even make the roster, let alone ever see the field.

Brady's father, Tom Sr., later recalled that the moment was "one of the most emotional and difficult days of Tom's life." He had spent years proving himself at Michigan, only to be overlooked by nearly every NFL team.

But instead of letting the disappointment consume him, Brady used it as fuel. He told himself that this was just another challenge.

Arriving in New England: The 199th Pick Walks Into Foxborough

A few weeks after the draft, Brady arrived at the Patriots' facility in Foxborough for rookie minicamp.

When he walked into the building, he wasn't seen as the future of the franchise. He was just another name on the roster, another late-round pick trying to fight for a job.

At the time, the Patriots had an established starting quarterback in Drew Bledsoe, who had signed a 10-year, $103 million contract extension that offseason. There was no competition for the starting job—Bledsoe was the guy.

Brady wasn't even second on the depth chart. He was fourth, behind Bledsoe, John Friesz, and Michael Bishop. He was aware that he would face a difficult challenge. However, he also knew the following: He had been overlooked before. He had fought through adversity at Michigan. He had proven people wrong his entire career. And he was ready to do it again.

The Totem Pole's Lowest Man Arrives in New England In Foxborough, Massachusetts, Tom Brady became a New England Patriot upon boarding the plane. But there was no grand introduction, no cameras waiting for him,

TOM BRADY BIOGRAPHY:

no press conference. He was a sixth-round pick, just another body in the locker room, a long shot to even make the team.

Brady took in everything as he entered the Patriots' facility. The weight room, the practice field, the offices—this was the NFL. This was where he had dreamed of playing. But there was not enough time to absorb everything. He was aware that he had work to do. The reality of his situation hit him quickly. The Patriots' franchise quarterback, Drew Bledsoe, was a seasoned pro. He was the highest-paid player in NFL history at the time because he had just signed a $103 million contract for ten years. There were two other quarterbacks in front of Bledsoe: John Friesz, a veteran backup with experience.

Michael Bishop, a mobile, athletic quarterback who had been a star at Kansas State.

And then, there was Brady—the fourth-string quarterback, a 199th pick nobody expected to last.

Brady wasn't just fighting for playing time. He was fighting for a roster spot. Most sixth-round picks never make it to the regular season. Many are cut before training camp even ends.

Brady knew he couldn't afford to blend in. He had to stand out.

First Impressions: A Young Kid with an Old Mindset

Brady's first interactions with the Patriots' staff set the tone for his entire career.

Shortly after he arrived, he met Robert Kraft, the owner of the New England Patriots.

Kraft, who had personally approved the drafting of Brady in the sixth round, didn't expect much from the young quarterback.

But when Brady introduced himself, he looked Kraft directly in the eye, shook his hand firmly, and said something that stuck with him forever:

"Mr. Kraft, I'm the best choice this company has ever made." It was a bold assertion. In the NFL, Brady had never played a down. He was just a scrawny kid from Michigan with an unimpressive combine performance.

But Kraft later admitted that he saw something different in Brady at that time. It wasn't arrogance. It was pure confidence.

When no one else did, Brady believed in his own abilities. Training Camp: Outworking Everyone

TOM BRADY BIOGRAPHY:

Brady was aware that he had to make every rep count when training camp started. He wasn't the most athletic. His arm strength wasn't elite. But he had something else—a relentless work ethic and unmatched preparation.

Brady showed up before sunrise every day. While other players were still asleep, he was in the film room, breaking down plays, studying defenses, and learning the Patriots' complex playbook.

By the time practice started, he already had a mental advantage over everyone else.

During drills, he wasn't flashy, but he was consistent. He didn't make mistakes. He didn't force bad throws. He played well, took advantage of what the defense gave him, and did the right thing. Brady's remarkable capacity for information retention was quickly recognized by coaches. He didn't just learn the plays—he understood them at a deeper level. He could read defenses, anticipate coverages, and make quick adjustments on the fly.

Still, he was buried on the depth chart.

Every practice rep was a battle. He wasn't getting as many snaps as Bledsoe or Friesz, but whenever he did get a chance, he made the most of it.

The Preseason: Brady's First Taste of NFL Action

During the 2000 preseason, Brady got his first real chance. The Patriots coaching staff wanted to evaluate him, but as a fourth-string quarterback, he wasn't going to get many chances.

When he finally got into a game, he didn't light up the stat sheet. His throws were crisp but conservative. He kept it safe. However, what stood out was his composure. He wasn't rattled. He didn't get scared. He seemed to belong there. Patriots offensive coordinator Charlie Weis took notice.

Weis wasn't completely sold on Brady's arm strength or athleticism, but he saw something different in him—a calm presence, a quick mind, and an unshakable confidence.

By the end of the preseason, Brady had climbed from fourth-string to third-string.

He was no longer at the very bottom. He had beaten out Michael Bishop for the final quarterback spot on the roster.

TOM BRADY BIOGRAPHY:

He wasn't going to start. He wasn't even the backup. But he had done enough to survive.

That was a victory in and of itself for a sixth-round selection. The Regular Season: Learning from the Sidelines

During the 2000 season, Brady didn't play a single meaningful snap. He spent the entire year watching, learning, and preparing.

But he didn't just go through the motions.

Every week, he prepared like he was the starter. He studied film obsessively. He took notes on everything—coverages, tendencies, blitz packages.

During games, he stood next to Charlie Weis with a clipboard, absorbing every detail. He watched how Bledsoe read defenses, how he made decisions, and how he adjusted at the line of scrimmage.

He also built relationships with his teammates.

Brady made an effort to connect with every player on the roster—not just the stars, but the backups, the special teams guys, even the practice squad players.

He wanted to be a leader.

Even though he was just a rookie, he carried himself like a veteran.

The End of the 2000 Season: A New Challenge Awaits

The Patriots finished the 2000 season with a disappointing 5-11 record. The team had a difficult year, and head coach Bill Belichick felt the pressure. After being promoted from defensive coordinator to head coach that year, the team had struggled. There were whispers that his job could be in danger if things didn't improve.

Brady, on the other hand, was a sideshow. Most people didn't expect him to ever play a significant role for the Patriots.

But inside the organization, something was shifting.

By the end of the season, Belichick and Weis had started to take notice.

They saw Brady's preparation. His leadership impressed them. They saw his ability to process information quickly.

He was still not prepared to lead the team. But they knew they had something in him.

As the season ended, Brady walked into the Patriots' offices for his exit interview.

TOM BRADY BIOGRAPHY:

In those meetings, the majority of quarterbacks on the third team received little attention. They were usually just told, "Good job, see you next year." But Brady didn't treat it that way. Instead, he walked up to Belichick and Weis and delivered a message that would define the rest of his career: "I'm going to show you why I ought to be your starting quarterback," I said. They didn't respond. They merely nodded. But deep inside, they knew Brady wasn't just another backup.

He was something different.

And soon, the entire world would find out.

TOM BRADY BIOGRAPHY:

CHAPTER FOUR: STEPPING IN, STEPPING UP

during the 2001 Season The unexpected turning point in the offseason Tom Brady was the third-string quarterback for the entire 2000 season, so he was aware that his time had not yet come. He had been patient, watching Drew Bledsoe lead the offense from the sidelines, studying every snap, and taking in information like a sponge. But patience wasn't enough—he needed to make the coaching staff believe in him.

Brady had one objective when the offseason of 2001 began: to demonstrate that he was more than just a backup. He transformed his body, working with the Patriots' strength and conditioning coaches to improve his overall athleticism. He had been lanky and unimpressive physically when he got out of college; now, he was building muscle, strengthening his arms, and improving his mechanics. But it wasn't just about his physical preparation. Mentally, he took a leap forward.

Brady treated the offseason as if he were the starter, rather than just another break. He spent countless hours in the film room, breaking down defenses, learning coverages, and mastering Charlie Weis' offense.

The majority of backup quarterbacks would have been satisfied to hold a clipboard. Brady wasn't.

Then something happened in training camp. The Quarterback Competition – Shocking the Patriots' Coaching Staff

During 2001 training camp, Brady arrived with a new presence, one that his teammates immediately noticed.

"Something was different about Tom," said Willie McGinest, one of the Patriots' veteran leaders. Even though he wasn't, "He carried himself like he was the guy." Brady was no longer an afterthought, even though Drew Bledsoe remained the undisputed starter. He was now the clear No. 2 quarterback, having overtaken John Friesz on the depth chart.

Although it may not seem like much, the Patriots' locker room experienced a seismic shift as a result. Belichick and Weis saw it too. Brady was no longer just a backup quarterback learning the system—he was executing it at a high level in practices and scrimmages.

Brady's accuracy stood out. He was doing more than just easy throws; he was also making passes with narrow windows, reading defenses faster

TOM BRADY BIOGRAPHY:

than before, and displaying poise that was beyond his experience. Brady was unquestionably, aside from Bledsoe, the best quarterback in camp when the preseason began. And then, in preseason games, something happened that changed everything.

Brady looked more efficient than Bledsoe.

It wasn't just the fact that he completed passes—it was how he did it. He controlled the offense precisely, moved the chains, and avoided making poor choices. Belichick paid attention. By the end of the preseason, Brady had solidified his spot as the team's No. 2 quarterback. He wasn't just a third-stringer anymore. He was now one play away from becoming the starter.

No one expected that opportunity to come so soon.

Week 2: The Moment That Changed NFL History

The Patriots opened the 2001 regular season with a loss to the Cincinnati Bengals, but no one was panicking. Drew Bledsoe was still their guy, and there was confidence that the team would bounce back.

Then, in Week 2, against the New York Jets, everything changed.

With five minutes left in the fourth quarter, the Patriots were trailing 10-3, and Bledsoe dropped back to pass. As he rolled out to his right, Jets linebacker Mo Lewis came flying in and delivered a crushing hit to Bledsoe's chest.

Bledsoe stumbled to the sideline, visibly shaken, but he stayed in the game. At the time, no one was aware that his injury was much worse than it appeared. He gave up and fell to the bench, struggling to breathe. Internal bleeding had begun, and within hours, he was rushed to the hospital.

That was it.

Tom Brady was forced into starting the game because Bledsoe was out for the season. The 199th pick in the draft was now leading the New England Patriots.

Brady's First Start: A Rocky Beginning

Brady made his NFL debut against the Indianapolis Colts in Week 3. The matchup was expected to be a disaster for New England—not only were they missing their franchise quarterback, but they were facing Peyton Manning, one of the best quarterbacks in the league.

TOM BRADY BIOGRAPHY:

But Brady didn't flinch.

He did exactly what Belichick and Weis wanted: he played smart, error-free football rather than trying to be a superstar. The Patriots leaned on their running game and defense, and Brady managed the game perfectly.

New England crushed the Colts 44-13, and suddenly, there was a new energy in Foxborough.

Growing Confidence: A New Leader Emerges

Brady wasn't lighting up the stat sheet, but he was doing something even more important: He was winning games.

His self-assurance increased with each game as he led the Patriots to victories over the Chargers, Dolphins, and Falcons. Veteran players—many of whom had been loyal to Bledsoe—began to rally around Brady.

The way he carried himself, the way he prepared, the way he never got rattled under pressure—they saw something in him that felt different.

By the time Week 10 rolled around, the Patriots were 5-4 and in the playoff hunt.

And then, the moment of truth arrived.

Bledsoe is allowed to return—a decision that affects the franchise Drew Bledsoe was finally allowed to play after recovering for weeks. Most expected him to return as the starting quarterback. After all, he was a legend of the franchise, a three-time Pro Bowler, and the team's face. But Bill Belichick had other plans.

Despite everything Bledsoe had done for the Patriots, Belichick made a bold, controversial decision:

He was sticking with Brady.

The move shocked the NFL world. How could Belichick bench Bledsoe for a second-year, sixth-round pick?

But Belichick saw what everyone else in the locker room saw—Brady was leading the team in a way that Bledsoe never had.

He wasn't just winning games—he was commanding the locker room, elevating the team, and refusing to be rattled by pressure.

With Brady under center, the Patriots won 11 of their last 14 games, finishing the season at 11-5.

TOM BRADY BIOGRAPHY:

They had done something unimaginable. They had made the playoffs with Tom Brady as their quarterback.

The Playoffs: The Birth of a Dynasty

In the AFC Divisional Round, the Patriots faced the Oakland Raiders in one of the most controversial games in NFL history—the "Tuck Rule Game."

With the Patriots trailing 13-10 in the final minutes, Brady was hit by Charles Woodson, causing a fumble that would have ended New England's season.

But after a review, officials ruled that Brady's arm was moving forward, making it an incomplete pass instead of a fumble.

The Patriots won on a field goal by Adam Vinatieri after maintaining possession and forcing overtime. From that moment on, it was clear—Brady wasn't just a backup filling in for Bledsoe. He was something special.

The Patriots defeated Pittsburgh in the AFC Championship, then shocked the world by beating the heavily favored St. Louis Rams in Super Bowl XXXVI.

A dynasty was born.

And it all started in 2001, with a sixth-round pick who refused to be overlooked.

Command, Changing the Locker Room By midseason, the Patriots weren't just winning games—they were rallying around Brady in a way no one had expected.

There had been initial hesitation. Drew Bledsoe had worked with many veterans for a long time. He had led the team to a Super Bowl appearance in 1996 and was considered one of the toughest quarterbacks in the league. His $103 million contract extension before the 2001 season had solidified his status as the face of the franchise.

However, Brady was altering culture. He was a leader who demanded excellence, not just a substitute. The Little Things That Made Brady Different

Brady worked harder than anyone. He showed up early at the facility, stayed late into the night, and treated each practice like a playoff game. Tedy Bruschi, Troy Brown, and Willie McGinest, three veterans who were

TOM BRADY BIOGRAPHY:

initially skeptical, started to buy in. "Tom didn't act like a backup. "We followed after he took command," Bruschi said later. What set him apart from Bledsoe? It wasn't strength or speed. Bledsoe had the stronger arm, was more experienced, and had already led multiple game-winning drives in his career.

But Brady had an unshakable mindset.

Even when things went wrong, he never panicked. He never let the moment overwhelm him.

His teammates began to have faith not only in the system but also in him. By November, the Patriots had won five of their last six games, and they weren't looking back.

versus Week 10 The Statement Game in Buffalo The Patriots played the Buffalo Bills on November 11, 2001, in a game that would define Brady's control over the team. The game was an absolute shootout.

Brady threw for four touchdowns and led the Patriots to a come-from-behind 21-11 victory.

It wasn't just that he played well—it was how he played.

When it mattered most, he stood in the pocket, took hits, and made crucial throws. The fact that this was now Brady's team was openly acknowledged by Patriots players after the game. The moment that made it official came next. Bledsoe's clearance to play in Week 11 was the Patriots' biggest decision ever. Drew Bledsoe was given the all-clear to play again after missing two months. The hypothesis? He'd take his job back.

But Bill Belichick saw things differently.

He watched Brady lead the Patriots to a 5-2 record since taking over. He saw how the locker room had come together in support of him. He had a decision to make.

He also succeeded on November 14, 2001. Brady remained the primary player. Bledsoe served as a backup. The move shocked the NFL.

Even Patriots fans and analysts couldn't believe it. How could Belichick bench a three-time Pro Bowl quarterback in favor of a sixth-round pick with only a handful of starts?

However, Belichick had no interest in resumes. He was focused on winning. Brady was winning.

So, Brady was the guy.

TOM BRADY BIOGRAPHY:

The Rest of the Regular Season – A Team Transformed

Belichick's decision proved to be the right one.

With Brady at the helm, the Patriots won six straight games to finish the regular season 11-5.

Brady wasn't just managing the game anymore—he was making plays that won games.

He threw a game-winning touchdown against the Jets, led a late comeback vs. the Dolphins, and proved he was ready for the biggest stage of all—the NFL Playoffs.

He was still not believed in by the world. They would soon find out. The Playoffs – The Birth of a Dynasty

AFC Divisional Round: The Tuck Rule Game – Brady's First Legendary Moment

On January 19, 2002, in a blizzard at Foxborough Stadium, the Patriots faced the Oakland Raiders.

It was one of the most controversial games in NFL history.

The Patriots were 13-10 down with less than two minutes left. Brady dropped back to pass, and just as he was about to throw, Charles Woodson hit him, knocking the ball loose.

The Raiders recovered. The game was over.

Or did it? After reviewing the play, the officials determined that Brady's arm was moving forward, indicating that the play was not a fumble but rather an incomplete pass. It was known as the Tuck Rule, and Raiders fans still believe they were robbed of their money. However, Brady was focused on winning rather than controversy. He led the Patriots into field goal range with ice in his veins. The game went into overtime after Adam Vinatieri made one of the most crucial field goals in NFL history, a 45-yarder through a swirling blizzard. Brady took control in OT, led another drive, and set up Vinatieri for another game-winning kick.

Final score: Patriots 16, Raiders 13.

The legend of Tom Brady had officially begun.

Brady's Validation and Bledsoe's Redemption in the AFC Championship Game In the AFC Championship Game, the Patriots will play the Pittsburgh Steelers. But early in the game, Brady took a hit to the knee and was forced to leave.

TOM BRADY BIOGRAPHY:

In a twist of fate, Drew Bledsoe came in and led the Patriots to victory.
After the game, Belichick had a choice to make.
Would he use Bledsoe, his most successful quarterback, again for the Super Bowl? Or would he stick with Brady?
He stuck with Brady.
It was one of the boldest moves in NFL history.
Super Bowl XXXVI – Brady Becomes a Champion
The Patriots entered Super Bowl XXXVI as massive underdogs against the St. Louis Rams, aka "The Greatest Show on Turf."
The Rams, led by Kurt Warner, had the most high-powered offense in the NFL.
Brady, on the other hand, was a rookie starter who had never played in a playoff game before. The Patriots weren't supposed to win.
But Brady had other plans.
With the game tied 17-17, the Patriots got the ball with 1:21 left.
Commentators expected them to run out the clock and play for overtime.
Instead, Brady led the Patriots with surgical precision down the field. With seven seconds left, Adam Vinatieri kicked the game-winning field goal.
Final score: Patriots 20, Rams 17.
The New England Patriots were Super Bowl champions.
And Tom Brady—a sixth-round pick who wasn't even supposed to make the roster—was the MVP.
The Moment That Changed Everything
After the game, Brady stood on the podium, holding the Lombardi Trophy.
A year earlier, no one knew his name. Now, he was a Super Bowl champion. And he was just getting started.

TOM BRADY BIOGRAPHY:

CHAPTER FIVE: PROVING IT WASN'T A FLUKE – BUILDING A DYNASTY

The Impact of Super Bowl XXXVI: A Revolutionary Franchise Every NFL player wants to win the Super Bowl, but Tom Brady and the New England Patriots found the experience to be surreal. Just over a year earlier, Brady had been a backup quarterback with no expectations. Now, he was the youngest Super Bowl-winning quarterback in NFL history at just 24 years old.

Brady raised the Lombardi Trophy with his signature childish grin as confetti fell inside the Louisiana Superdome. But there was an insatiable hunger hidden behind that smile. Winning one Super Bowl was an incredible accomplishment. But demonstrating that it wasn't a fluke? That was something completely different. The football community remained skeptical. A lot of analysts thought that the Patriots had caught lightning in a bottle and that their run to the Super Bowl had been fueled by luck rather than long-term greatness. The "Tuck Rule" controversy against the Raiders, Drew Bledsoe stepping in during the AFC Championship, and an underdog win against the heavily favored Rams—all of it added to the perception that New England had simply been lucky.

The actual test was coming up. Could the Patriots and Brady demonstrate that they were not a one-hit wonder team? There's no time to celebrate in the offseason. The majority of players are entitled to time off during the offseason if they win a Super Bowl. Brady not Almost as soon as the Super Bowl parade ended, Brady was back in the weight room, studying film, and preparing for the next season.

"Winning the Super Bowl is great," Brady told reporters, "but that was last season. These victories are no longer considered. That mindset shocked some of his teammates. Brady wasn't satisfied.

Together with Patriots strength coach Mike Woicik, he worked harder than ever to improve his footwork, strengthen his arms, and become more durable. What is his main focus? Becoming the undisputed leader of the team.

TOM BRADY BIOGRAPHY:

During the 2001 season, Brady had been the young quarterback filling in for an injured Bledsoe. Even after winning the Super Bowl, some players still saw Bledsoe as the true franchise leader.

Brady wanted to erase all doubt.

2002 Season – A Rocky Start

With a championship ring on their fingers, the Patriots entered the 2002 season with sky-high expectations.

But the hard reality hit. After opening the season with a dominant 30-14 win over the Pittsburgh Steelers, the Patriots lost four straight games, dropping to 3-4.

Brady was doing well, but the team had problems with injuries, bad defense, and bad offensive play. The pressure started to mount. Was the Super Bowl win a one-year wonder?

Would Brady be exposed as a flash in the pan?

Adversity Breeds Resilience – Brady's First True Test as a Leader

Brady's leadership abilities were put to the test like never before during the losing streak. The veteran players were disappointed. The media was questioning if the Patriots had been a fluke.

A lot of quarterbacks might have given up at this point. Brady didn't. Instead, he rallied the team.

After a loss to Denver in Week 9, Brady addressed the team in a closed-door meeting. He made it abundantly clear to them that it was unacceptable to lose. Brady stated, "You don't just get to be a Super Bowl champion forever." "You have to go out and earn it—every single game."

His passion was evident, and his teammates responded.

Midseason Turnaround – The Leader Emerges

Brady and the Patriots came back strong, winning their next three games, including a thrilling overtime victory of 26-20 over the Oakland Raiders, the same team they had defeated in the infamous Tuck Rule Game the year before. A victory made a statement. Brady demonstrated his growing self-assurance and command of the offense by throwing for 300 yards and two touchdowns. New England was back in the playoff race.

A Disappointing Finish – Missing the Playoffs by Inches

Despite their midseason resurgence, the Patriots finished the year 9-7, narrowly missing the playoffs due to tiebreakers.

TOM BRADY BIOGRAPHY:

It was a disappointing season. But for Brady, it was the greatest learning experience of his career.

He realized that winning in the NFL wasn't about one magical season—it was about sustained excellence.

Brady returned to Foxborough in the offseason with a new purpose: Building a dynasty.

2003 Season – The Birth of a Dynasty

Something was different about Brady in 2003.

He was more confident, more in control, and more ruthless in his preparation.

When the Patriots started the season 2-2, critics started whispering again. Then, Brady and the Patriots went on a winning streak for the ages.

They won 12 straight games to finish the season 14-2—the best record in franchise history.

Brady was no longer just a game manager. He was making clutch throws, leading game-winning drives, and proving he could carry a team.

The Patriots stormed into the playoffs and dominated the Indianapolis Colts in the AFC Championship Game.

Brady had outdueled Peyton Manning again, cementing his reputation as a clutch performer.

Super Bowl XXXVIII – The Game That Silenced the Doubters

In Super Bowl XXXVIII, Brady and the Patriots faced the Carolina Panthers. It was a back-and-forth battle, but in the final moments, with the game tied 29-29, Brady got the ball.

With 1:08 left on the clock, he led a textbook game-winning drive, setting up Adam Vinatieri's championship-clinching field goal.

Final score: Patriots 32, Panthers 29.

For the second time in three years, the Patriots were Super Bowl champions.

Brady had silenced every critic.

Back-to-Back Champions – The 2004 Season

Now, the question wasn't whether Brady was good.

The question was: Could he build a dynasty?

He responded with a resounding "yes" in 2004. The Patriots went 14-2 again, dominating their way through the regular season.

TOM BRADY BIOGRAPHY:

Brady was now undeniably one of the best quarterbacks in football.
He led the Patriots to another playoff run, defeating Peyton Manning and the Colts again before taking down the Philadelphia Eagles in Super Bowl XXXIX.
With a third championship in four years, the Patriots were officially an NFL dynasty.
Brady, also? He was no longer the kid who replaced Bledsoe. He was the best quarterback in the NFL.
The Dynasty Was Only Getting Started By the end of the 2004 season, Brady had done something no quarterback in modern NFL history had done—won three Super Bowls in just four seasons as a starter.
He had gone from a sixth-round pick no one believed in to the face of the greatest football dynasty of the 21st century. But for Brady, it still wasn't enough. He wanted more than just three rings. He wanted more.
And over the next decade, he would prove that his greatness was only just beginning.
The Tension of Upholding a Title Winning a Super Bowl puts a target on a team's back. Every opponent wants to beat the defending champions, and every game feels like a playoff battle.
The Patriots' 2002 campaign served as a reminder of how difficult it is to maintain dominance. The previous year had been magical, like a Cinderella tale that overcame all obstacles. However, they were now the ones being hunted, not the hunters. Brady was no longer Drew Bledsoe's untested replacement. He was now a Super Bowl MVP, and defenses were beginning to game-plan specifically for him.
Bill Belichick knew that complacency was the enemy.
"You can't win on last year's success," he told the team before the season started. "You have to prove it all over again."
Those words meant a lot to Brady. A More Confident, More Assertive Brady
Brady entered the 2002 season with a new sense of confidence.
He was no longer deferring to veteran leaders—he was the leader.
Teammates saw the difference. He was more vocal in the huddle, demanding perfection on every snap.

TOM BRADY BIOGRAPHY:

Brady's competitive fire burned hotter than ever. He obsessed over film study, analyzing defensive schemes with a level of detail that surprised even Belichick.

"Tom prepared like a 10-year veteran," said offensive coordinator Charlie Weis. "He wasn't satisfied just being good—he wanted to be great."

But greatness isn't achieved overnight.

The harsh reality of defending a title: early struggles The Patriots were successful in their first three games of the 2002 season. Brady was performing well, throwing for more than 300 yards in each of those victories. The Patriots looked like they hadn't lost a step.

Then everything broke down. A Week 4 loss to the San Diego Chargers was a wake-up call. The Patriots were dominated 21-14, and Brady struggled against a relentless pass rush.

That loss was followed by three more defeats in a row. Suddenly, the Patriots were 3-4, and the same media that had questioned their Super Bowl legitimacy was piling on.

How Brady Handled the Doubters

Brady received severe criticism for the first time in his career. Some analysts suggested, "Maybe he's just a one-year wonder." Others argued that "Maybe Bledsoe was the better long-term option." Brady didn't say anything publicly. He let his work speak for him.

After the fourth straight loss, he gathered the team together in the locker room.

"This isn't who we are," he told them. "We worked too hard to let this season slip away."

The locker room was ignited by Brady's passion. In response, the Patriots won four games in a row, including a thrilling overtime victory over the Raiders in a rematch of the infamous Tuck Rule Game from the previous season. The tragic conclusion to 2002 The Patriots' playoff hopes hinged on their matchup with the Miami Dolphins in Week 17, despite their turnaround in the middle of the season. Brady delivered in the clutch, leading a last-minute drive to tie the game and force overtime. Adam Vinatieri's field goal secured the win.

But it wasn't enough.

TOM BRADY BIOGRAPHY:

Because of tiebreakers, the Patriots missed the playoffs—a devastating end to their title defense.

For Brady, it was a bitter pill to swallow. But rather than dwelling on disappointment, he used it as fuel.

The Development of a Champion: A Determining Offseason Brady didn't take a vacation that offseason.

He, on the other hand, worked tirelessly to improve his game. Belichick and Weis designed a more aggressive offensive system, one that gave Brady more control at the line of scrimmage.

Brady also added muscle to his frame, determined to withstand the punishment of a full season.

It was going to be different in 2003. Brady wasn't just trying to win another Super Bowl. He was out to prove that the Patriots were not a one-hit wonder.

The 2003 Season – A Team on a Mission

The Patriots started 2-2, and the media began questioning them again. Then, something clicked.

Brady and the Patriots went on a winning streak of 12 games and went 14-2, which was the best record in the franchise's history. Brady had developed into a true field general, the offense was more explosive, and the defense was in control. His ability to make pre-snap reads and adjust at the line of scrimmage had taken a massive leap forward.

Weis stated, "We weren't just running plays." "Tom was leading the charge." In the AFC Championship Game, the Patriots defeated Peyton Manning and the Colts by a score of 0-3. Super Bowl XXXVIII – The Game That Defined Brady's Clutch Gene

On February 1, 2004, the Patriots faced the Carolina Panthers in Super Bowl XXXVIII.

It turned into one of the most thrilling Super Bowls in history.

The game was tied 29-29 with just over a minute left.

Brady was under pressure because the Panthers had just scored. He didn't flinch.

Adam Vinatieri's game-winning field goal was set up by Brady as he carefully marched the Patriots down the field, completing five passes in a row. Final score: Patriots 32, Panthers 29.

TOM BRADY BIOGRAPHY:

After three years, Brady had won his second Super Bowl. And this time, there were no more doubts.

Cementing the Dynasty in 2004 Brady and the Patriots weren't satisfied with two rings. In 2004, they were even better.

They won another 14 games, tied an NFL record with 21 straight wins dating back to the previous season, and steamrolled their way to another Super Bowl.

Brady once more delivered in the most crucial situations. In Super Bowl XXXIX against the Philadelphia Eagles, he threw for 236 yards and 2 touchdowns, leading the Patriots to a 24-21 victory.

It was their third championship in four years—an achievement not seen since the 1990s Dallas Cowboys.

Conclusion: From Football's Underdog to Icon Brady wasn't just a good quarterback by 2004. He was a legend in the making.

The Patriots had built a dynasty, and Brady had gone from a sixth-round draft pick to a three-time Super Bowl champion before the age of 28. But he wasn't done yet.

Because in his mind, the best was still to come.

TOM BRADY BIOGRAPHY:

CHAPTER SIX: THE PERFECT SEASON THAT WASN'T – 2007 AND THE 18-1 HEARTBREAK

New Beginnings in New England: The Offseason of 2007 After winning three Super Bowls in four years, the Patriots were already regarded as one of the greatest dynasties in NFL history. However, their last championship had come in the 2004 season, and the following two years ended in disappointment.

In 2005, they were eliminated in the divisional round by the Denver Broncos. The 2006 season was an improvement, as they made it to the AFC Championship Game, but a second-half collapse against the Indianapolis Colts ended their Super Bowl hopes.

This was insufficient for Tom Brady. Despite being a three-time champion and two-time Super Bowl MVP, he had never had a truly dominant statistical season. The Patriots' offensive strategy had always been well-balanced, relying on a strong running game and a defense that could win close games. Although Brady had performed admirably, he had not produced the jaw-dropping numbers of Peyton Manning or other quarterbacks. That was about to change.

The Patriots completely revamped their offense in the 2007 offseason. They traded for Randy Moss, one of the most talented wide receivers in NFL history, and signed Wes Welker, a shifty slot receiver who would become one of Brady's favorite targets. They also added Donte' Stallworth to stretch the field and tight end Benjamin Watson to give Brady more red-zone options.

Brady used all of his weapons for the first time in his career. The outcomes would be unprecedented. The First Signs of Greatness – A Dominant Start to 2007

From the very first game of the 2007 season, it was clear that this Patriots team was different.

They defeated the New York Jets 38-14 in Week 1. Brady threw for 297 yards and three touchdowns, two of which went to Randy Moss. It was their most dominant opening performance in years, and it set the tone for what was to come.

Week after week, the Patriots demolished opponents.

TOM BRADY BIOGRAPHY:

They were making teams look bad, not just winning games. Week 2: Patriots 38, Chargers 14

Week 3: Bills 7, Patriots 38 Week 4: Patriots 34, Bengals 13

Brady was playing at an MVP level, throwing for multiple touchdowns every week.

The Patriots were 8-0 at midseason, and Brady had already thrown for 30 touchdowns. The NFL had never seen an offense this explosive.

Brady and Moss' Unstoppable Connection While the entire Patriots offense was thriving, the connection between Brady and Randy Moss was on another level.

Moss had been labeled as a troubled player before coming to New England. After early success with the Minnesota Vikings, he had spent two frustrating years in Oakland, where his motivation was questioned.

But in New England, Moss found the perfect quarterback.

He was a receiver Brady had never played with who could outjump and outrun any defender in the red zone. Instantaneous chemistry ensued.

Week 5 vs. Browns: Moss caught two more touchdowns, bringing his total to seven in just five games.

Week 8 versus Redskins: Moss had three touchdowns in one half as the Patriots won 52-7.

Week 9 vs. Colts: Moss caught a crucial pass for 55 yards to help the Patriots recover and stay undefeated. By the end of the regular season, Moss had caught 23 touchdown passes, breaking Jerry Rice's single-season record.

Brady, also? He had surpassed Peyton Manning's previous record of 49 touchdown passes by throwing 50 of them. The Patriots became the first team since the Miami Dolphins in 1972 to finish the regular season undefeated, going 16-0. But they weren't just undefeated—they were dominant.

Each game, they won by more than 19 points on average. No one could stop them.

Or so they thought.

A Different Kind of Challenge: The Playoffs The Patriots entered the playoffs as overwhelming favorites. Many believed they would cruise to a

TOM BRADY BIOGRAPHY:

Super Bowl victory and cement themselves as the greatest team in NFL history.

However, the playoffs introduced a new level of competition. In the divisional round, they faced the Jacksonville Jaguars. Brady completed 26 of 28 passes in a 31-20 victory over the Jaguars, one of his best performances ever. The Jaguars played tough, but Brady played well. In the AFC Championship, they met the San Diego Chargers, who were without their star quarterback Philip Rivers (who played injured). Brady was forced to throw three interceptions by the Chargers' defense, but the Patriots still won 21-12 thanks to a strong running game and a tough defense. Brady and the Patriots were now one win away from perfection.

Super Bowl XLII – The 18-1 Nightmare

On February 3, 2008, the Patriots faced the New York Giants in Super Bowl XLII.

The Giants had barely made the playoffs as a wild card team but had gained momentum, upsetting the Cowboys and Packers to reach the Super Bowl.

Most experts expected the Patriots to win easily.

After all, they had defeated the Giants 38-35 in Week 17 to complete their perfect season.

However, this game would be unique. A Combative Struggle From the opening snap, it was clear that the Giants' defense had a plan.

Led by Michael Strahan, Justin Tuck, and Osi Umenyiora, they attacked Brady relentlessly.

Despite protecting Brady throughout the year, the Patriots' offensive line struggled against the pass rush of the Giants. Brady took a lot of blows and never seemed at ease in the pocket. Still, the game remained low-scoring.

Brady's touchdown pass to Randy Moss gave the Patriots a 7-3 lead going into the fourth quarter. It appeared as though they might survive. The Helmet Catch – A Moment That Changed History

With just over two minutes remaining, the Giants faced 3rd and 5 from their own 44-yard line.

Eli Manning took the snap and was immediately pressured by the Patriots' defense.

TOM BRADY BIOGRAPHY:

He got away somehow and threw the ball far down the field. David Tyree, a little-known Giants receiver, jumped up and pinned the ball against his helmet while being tackled by Rodney Harrison.

It was one of the most unbelievable plays in Super Bowl history.

That play kept the Giants' drive alive, and just a few plays later, Plaxico Burress caught the game-winning touchdown.

Final score: Giants 17, Patriots 14.

The Fallout – A Stunned Brady and a Shattered Dream

Brady walked off the field in disbelief.

After 18 straight wins, they had fallen one game short of perfection.

The loss was devastating.

Players sat silently in the locker room, unable to comprehend what had transpired. For Brady, this was the most painful moment of his career.

He had set records, led the greatest offense the NFL had ever seen, and come within seconds of immortality—only to have it ripped away.

Moving Forward – The Fire Wasn't Out Yet

Many wondered how Brady and the Patriots would respond.

Would they ever be able to get over this setback? Brady had one response: put in more effort. He would never forget the 18-1 campaign, but it also served as fuel. Because for Brady, his story wasn't finished yet.

And the next chapter would be one of the greatest comebacks in sports history.

The Immediate Effects of Losing the Super Bowl After Super Bowl XLII, the Patriots' locker room was unlike any other under Bill Belichick. The air was thick with silence, broken only by the occasional deep sigh or the sound of tape being ripped off cleats. Players sat motionless, staring at the ground, trying to process the shock of losing a game they were expected to win.

Tom Brady, who had always been the heart of the team, sat at his locker in disbelief. His uniform was still on, his jersey stained with the turf of University of Phoenix Stadium, his body battered from the relentless Giants' pass rush. He had taken five sacks and been hit countless times.

For Brady, it wasn't just the loss that hurt—it was how close they had come. He had seemingly sealed their perfect 19-0 season by delivering to Randy Moss what should have been the game-winning touchdown just minutes earlier. But football is a game of inches and moments, and David

TOM BRADY BIOGRAPHY:

Tyree's miraculous Helmet Catch had rewritten history in the cruelest way possible.

Never one to give lengthy speeches, Bill Belichick simply informed his team: "This one is going to hurt. It should hurt. But you need to decide what you do with that pain."

The defeat not only hurt, but it also changed Brady and the Patriots forever. Coping with the Loss: Brady's Internal Battle Brady had never lost like this before, despite the fact that he had always been an emotional competitor. Every championship he had won had come in close, dramatic fashion—he knew what it felt like to be on the winning side of a last-second Super Bowl victory.

Now, for the first time, he was on the other side.

The week after the game, Brady barely slept. He replayed every moment in his mind:

What if he had been able to step up in the pocket just a half-second earlier on that final drive?

What if he had recognized the Giants' defensive adjustments sooner?

What if they had taken a different approach to blocking New York's pass rush?

He kept asking himself, Did I do enough?

His family, including Gisele Bündchen, tried to console him, but Brady wasn't ready to move on. He had spent the entire 2007 season rewriting the NFL record books, only for everything to vanish in a flash. The media came in waves. Some headlines called the Patriots "the biggest choke in sports history." Others questioned whether the Giants' game plan had made Brady and Belichick vulnerable. This was different from the criticism Brady was used to receiving. This was his defining season, and the final chapter had been ripped away.

The Patriots' Offseason – A Team Searching for Redemption

The Patriots' 2008 offseason began in an unfamiliar place: disappointment. In previous years, their offseasons were filled with celebrations, championship parades, and plans for defending their Super Bowl titles. This time, it was about putting the pieces back together. The loss had also put a target on Bill Belichick's coaching methods. The Patriots had already

TOM BRADY BIOGRAPHY:

been dealing with the Spygate scandal earlier in the season, and now, with their Super Bowl loss, critics argued that Belichick's legacy was tarnished.
Internally, the Patriots' front office debated how to approach the next season.
Should they rebuild and retool the offense?
Or should they double down and try to repeat their dominant 2007 formula?
One thing was clear: Brady wasn't satisfied.
Brady's Response – A Ruthless Drive for Perfection
Tom Brady had always been known for his obsessive work ethic, but in the months following the Super Bowl loss, his dedication reached another level.
He spent countless hours in the film room, dissecting every detail of the Super Bowl loss.
He worked with offensive coordinator Josh McDaniels to identify ways to counteract the type of pass rush the Giants had used against them.
He threw hundreds of passes a day to his receivers, particularly Randy Moss and Wes Welker, determined to improve their timing even more.
Brady was now more than just trying to be great; he was desperate to get his life back on track. The 2008 Season – A Cruel Twist of Fate
The Patriots had one objective going into the 2008 season: to finish what they started. Brady walked into training camp with an icy determination. He spoke little about the previous season, but his actions spoke volumes.
In practice, he was sharper than ever, pushing his teammates to match his intensity. Players whispered that Brady was playing with a new kind of anger—not at them, but at himself for coming up short.
Then, in Week 1, disaster struck.
Brady dropped back to pass early in the first quarter against the Kansas City Chiefs in the season opener. As he stepped into his throw, Chiefs safety Bernard Pollard dove into his knee.
Brady crumpled to the ground, clutching his leg.
Silence fell over Gillette Stadium.
Everyone knew it immediately: something was seriously wrong.
Brady had torn his ACL and MCL, ending his season before it had even truly begun.
The Mental Toll of the Injury

TOM BRADY BIOGRAPHY:

For Brady, this was worse than losing the Super Bowl.
He had spent the entire offseason preparing for redemption, only to have it taken away in an instant.
Lying in his hospital bed after surgery, he felt helpless.
For the first time in his career, he wouldn't be in control.
His Patriots teammates had to play without him throughout the season. Backup quarterback Matt Cassel stepped in and led the team to an impressive 11-5 record, but they missed the playoffs due to tiebreakers.
Watching from the sidelines, Brady felt like an outsider.
He had unfinished business, but now he had to wait.
Using the Pain as Fuel – The Road to Redemption
The rehabilitation process was hard. Brady spent months rebuilding strength in his leg, working with physical therapists for hours each day.
Doctors warned that some quarterbacks never fully recovered from ACL tears.
Brady refused to believe that.
He watched film every day, treating rehab like game preparation.
He visualized himself back on the field, determined to make his return even greater.
He took inspiration from players like Jerry Rice by studying how other athletes had recovered from injuries similar to his own. He needed to get back to the field.
Because in his mind, the story wasn't over.
The Pain That Shaped the Future
The 2007 Patriots will always be remembered as one of the greatest teams in NFL history that fell just short of perfection.
That season permanently altered Brady. The Super Bowl loss and his 2008 injury reignited his hunger, proving that even after three championships, he still had something to prove.
And when he finally returned in 2009, he wasn't just playing to win games. He was playing to rewrite history.

TOM BRADY BIOGRAPHY:

CHAPTER SEVEN: THE INJURY of 2008: A CAREER IN PERIL THE MOMENT THAT CHANGED EVERYTHING

Retribution was supposed to be the theme of the 2008 season. In the waning moments of Super Bowl XLII, the Patriots were heartbreakingly close to achieving perfection after coming so close the year before. Tom Brady had spent the entire offseason fueling himself with that disappointment, determined to come back even stronger.

When he stepped onto the field at Gillette Stadium on September 7, 2008, for the Patriots' season opener against the Kansas City Chiefs, there was a quiet confidence in the air. Excited to see Brady and his high-powered offense return, fans packed the stands. That optimism was quickly dashed after just a few games. Brady dropped back early in the first quarter for a routine pass. He scanned the field, planted his foot, and prepared to step into his throw. Bernard Pollard, a Chiefs safety, lunged at him and dived low as he released the ball. Brady's left knee came into contact with Pollard's helmet. Brady crumpled to the ground instantly. At first, the stadium fell silent. Then a collective gasp rippled through the crowd. The on-field players froze and stared at their deceased quarterback. In pain, Brady grabbed his knee. He didn't get up.

The Aftermath – The Patriots' Worst Fear Confirmed

The field was flooded with trainers. Brady attempted to move his leg, but he was unable to support any weight. Bill Belichick, typically stone-faced on the sidelines, had an expression of quiet concern.

Brady was helped to the sideline, where doctors examined his knee. A few minutes later, he was carted to the locker room.

The game continued, with backup quarterback Matt Cassel taking over, but the Patriots were already bracing for the worst.

No one was happy when the game ended, with New England winning 17-10. The condition of Brady was the sole focus. That evening, Brady underwent an MRI scan. The results confirmed a torn ACL and MCL in his left knee.

His time here was up. The news sent shockwaves through the NFL. Just months earlier, Brady had shattered records, throwing 50 touchdown passes and leading one of the greatest offenses in history. He would not

TOM BRADY BIOGRAPHY:

take another snap for the remainder of the year at this point. His football career was about to begin with uncertainty. Brady's Initial Reaction – A New Kind of Challenge

When the doctors told Brady the extent of his injury, he refused to accept it at first.

"No. I'll be back before the season ends," he insisted.

But the reality was undeniable. ACL tears typically required 9 to 12 months of recovery, meaning he wouldn't be ready until at least the 2009 season.

For someone as competitive as Brady, the idea of sitting out an entire year was unthinkable.

As he left the doctor's office, Brady felt something he hadn't felt since he was an unproven quarterback fighting for a chance at Michigan—fear.

Not just fear of missing a season, but fear of never being the same player again.

The Psychological Toll – Doubts Begin to Creep In

Brady had always prided himself on being tough. He had played through sprained ankles, broken ribs, concussions, and countless other minor injuries over the years. But this was different.

For the first time, his body had failed him completely.

As he lay in bed that night, staring at the ceiling, the questions flooded his mind:

Will I ever be as good as I was before?

What if I am unable to move in the same manner? What if this is the first step toward the end? Brady had built his career on his relentless preparation and drive, but he had never faced an obstacle like this before.

The Surgery – A Complication That Made Things Worse

A few days later, Brady underwent surgery to repair his ACL and MCL. The procedure was considered routine, but within weeks, things took a turn for the worse.

Brady developed an infection in his knee, a serious complication that required multiple additional procedures. The infection had the potential to prolong his recovery time and, in extreme cases, even end a player's career. For the first time, the unthinkable seemed possible—Brady might never play football again.

TOM BRADY BIOGRAPHY:

This wasn't just about healing anymore. It was about survival.

The Patriots Without Brady – A Season of Uncertainty

While Brady was confined to hospital visits and physical therapy, the Patriots had to move forward without him.

Backup quarterback Matt Cassel, who hadn't started a game since high school, was thrust into the spotlight.

Few believed Cassel could keep the Patriots competitive, but he surprised everyone.

He led the team to an 11-5 record, proving that New England was still a formidable team even without its superstar quarterback.

He earned the respect of the entire league by throwing for more than 3,600 yards and 21 touchdowns. The Patriots were eliminated from the playoffs due to a tiebreaker, despite Cassel's success. It was a painful reminder of just how much Brady meant to the franchise.

Brady's Rehab – Rebuilding from the Ground Up

While the Patriots played their season without him, Brady was in the toughest battle of his career—not against an opponent, but against his own body.

Rehab was slow and painful.

At first, even walking without pain was difficult.

Basic movements—stepping, turning, bending his knee—required endless repetitions just to regain normal function.

Doctors warned him to be patient, but patience was never Brady's strength.

Brady attacked rehab like he attacked football preparation.

He worked with Alex Guerrero, his longtime trainer, to rebuild his strength and mobility.

He focused on every detail, from his diet to his flexibility, ensuring that his knee healed properly.

He studied film obsessively, refusing to let a year off dull his mental sharpness.

But doubt still lingered.

There were moments in rehab when his knee didn't feel right, moments where he wondered if he would ever be the same player again.

Yet, every time doubt crept in, Brady pushed harder.

TOM BRADY BIOGRAPHY:

The Turning Point – A Glimpse of the Old Brady

By early 2009, Brady was back on the field, slowly working his way toward full strength. One day during a throwing session, he uncorked a deep pass that spiraled perfectly through the air, landing right in his receiver's hands.

It was the first time since his injury that he felt like himself again.

The fire that had momentarily dimmed inside him was reignited. Brady realized that he wasn't just coming back—he was coming back stronger.

The Lessons Learned in 2008: A New Brady Emerges By the time the 2009 season arrived, Brady wasn't just recovered—he was reborn.

The injury had forced him to rethink everything:

His training methods became more refined.

His mental approach became even sharper.

His appreciation for the game deepened.

Brady had always played with a chip on his shoulder, but now he had something even greater—perspective.

He had faced the possibility of never playing again and had fought his way back.

He wasn't just playing for championships anymore.

He was playing because he knew how easily it could be taken away.

And with that new mindset, he was ready to write the next chapter—one that would define the second half of his legendary career. Tom Brady was forced, for the first time in his NFL career, to observe the Patriots' season without him. Sundays were strange. He wasn't in the huddle, calling plays. He was not collaborating with Bill Belichick to plan on the sidelines. Instead, he was at home, rehabbing his knee and trying to cope with an entirely new reality.

For an athlete who thrived on routine, the sudden change was jarring.

His daily schedule had always revolved around game preparation—practices, film sessions, weight training, and meetings. His life now consisted of slow, monotonous rehabilitation exercises. Despite the fact that he never sulked, Brady felt the weight of his isolation. He missed the camaraderie in the locker room, the excitement of a live game, and the experience of leading his team at a crucial time. Watching the Patriots play without him was frustrating. He wanted to be there, but there was nothing he could do.

TOM BRADY BIOGRAPHY:

The world of football moved on without him, and that reality was difficult to accept.

Matt Cassel's Success – A Mixed Emotion for Brady

Even though Brady wanted his team to win, there was a part of him that didn't like the idea of having another quarterback run the offense. Matt Cassel, a career backup, wasn't supposed to be able to replace Brady.

But something unexpected happened as the season went on: Cassel started to play well. Cassel gained self-assurance under Belichick's guidance. He began making smart decisions, running the Patriots' offense efficiently, and keeping the team in playoff contention.

While Brady was overjoyed for Cassel, he was also filled with fear. What if the Patriots learned to win without him?

What if Belichick realized he didn't need Brady to run his system?

What would happen to him in New England if this injury was the beginning of the end? It wasn't an irrational fear. In the NFL, you're only valuable until someone else can do your job.

Brady had witnessed it before. In 2001, he succeeded Drew Bledsoe and never returned to the position. Now, Cassel was playing well, and some were wondering if Brady was replaceable.

He was terrified by the thought. Rebuilding His Body – The Most Intense Training of His Career

While Brady had always been preoccupied with preparation, rehab required a new level of discipline. Relearning how to move was part of the process, not just strengthening his knee. His trainer, Alex Guerrero, was at his side every day, pushing him to regain his explosiveness. Guerrero's unconventional training methods, which emphasized flexibility, muscle pliability, and resistance-based movements, became Brady's new obsession.

Every morning began with deep tissue therapy, helping to loosen his scar tissue.

In order to ensure that his knee could withstand the demands of a full NFL season, he spent hours practicing balance and stability. He studied biomechanics, analyzing every step of his throwing motion to ensure he didn't develop bad habits while compensating for his injury.

The goal wasn't just to recover—it was to come back better than before.

TOM BRADY BIOGRAPHY:

The outside world's doubts While Brady worked in silence, the outside world was buzzing with speculation.

Some experts questioned whether he would ever be the same player again.

Others pointed to the history of quarterbacks with major knee injuries—many never returned to their peak form.

If Cassel continued to thrive, there were rumblings that the Patriots might consider trading him. Brady refused to let the doubt affect him.

He was probably fueled by it. He had built his career on proving people wrong, and this was just another challenge.

The Mental Battle – Overcoming Fear

As his knee got stronger, another obstacle emerged—fear.

Would his knee hold up in a real game? Given the possibility of being hit by a defender, would he hesitate to enter a throw? Would he ever trust his body the way he once did?

One of the hardest parts of rehab wasn't just fixing his knee—it was convincing himself that he was still the same quarterback.

For months, Brady worked on erasing that fear.

He practiced with controlled contact, testing his ability to step into pressure. He forced himself to take hits in training sessions, reminding his body that he could withstand the impact.

The process was slow, but gradually, the fear began to fade.

By the time he was cleared for full practice, Brady had one goal in mind: Prove that he was still the best quarterback in the NFL.

Brady's hushed retaliation in the offseason of 2009 As the 2009 season approached, all eyes were on Brady.

Would he still qualify as elite? Would the Patriots still be a threat to win the Super Bowl? Or would he struggle, proving that the injury had taken away his greatness?

Brady didn't talk about it much. He let his actions speak instead.

In private workouts, he looked sharper than ever.

His arm strength had returned.

His mobility was improving, though he was never going to be a scrambling quarterback.

TOM BRADY BIOGRAPHY:

He had eliminated any hesitation in his movements, showing that his confidence was back.

He was ready.

Cassel's Departure – The Patriots Reaffirm Their Trust in Brady

While Brady was preparing for his return, the Patriots made a major decision—they traded Matt Cassel to the Kansas City Chiefs.

It was a clear message:

This was still Brady's team.

Despite Cassel's strong 2008 season, the Patriots never wavered in their belief that Brady was their franchise quarterback. The trade was a sign of faith, but it also put even more pressure on Brady to prove them right.

The Preseason – A Statement of Intent

Brady's first live-action snaps in preseason games were crucial. Would he look rusty? Would he be hesitant? Would his knee hold up?

The answers came quickly.

In his first game back, Brady led the Patriots on a touchdown drive, completing crisp passes and commanding the offense as if he had never left.

His teammates noticed immediately—he was still the same guy.

That moment set the tone for the 2009 season.

Brady wasn't just back—he was out to prove something.

The 2009 Season Opener – A Hollywood Comeback

Tom Brady played in the Patriots' season opener against the Buffalo Bills on September 14, 2009, almost exactly one year after his injury. The energy in Gillette Stadium was electric.

Fans had waited a full year for this moment, and they erupted in cheers as Brady jogged onto the field.

The Patriots struggled for the majority of the game. The Bills led 24-13 with just five minutes left.

Then, Brady did what he had always done best—he led a comeback.

He threw two touchdown passes in the final minutes, securing a 25-24 win in dramatic fashion.

It was a fitting return. Tom Brady was not simply returning to the field when he left it. He was better than ever.

TOM BRADY BIOGRAPHY:

The concluding section of Brady's legacy is defining. The 2008 injury could have ended Brady's career. Many quarterbacks never recover fully from an ACL tear. Some never play again.

However, Brady had used the setback as fuel. He had reinvented his training, strengthened his mental game, and emerged with an even greater appreciation for football.

This wasn't the beginning of the end—it was the start of a new chapter.

The next phase of Brady's career wouldn't just be about winning.

It would be about defying expectations, rewriting history, and demonstrating that overcoming even the most difficult obstacles is possible.

TOM BRADY BIOGRAPHY:

CHAPTER EIGHT: A HISTORIC PARTNERSHIP IN THE BRADY-BELICHICK ERA

The Origins of a Legendary Partnership
When Tom Brady was drafted by the New England Patriots in the sixth round of the 2000 NFL Draft, few people could have predicted the historic partnership that would form between him and head coach Bill Belichick.
Belichick had a mixed reputation as a coach at the time. He had spent five seasons as the head coach of the Cleveland Browns, compiling a 36-44 record before being fired. His ability to lead a team was questioned, despite his reputation as a defensive genius. Brady, on the other hand, was an unknown backup quarterback—an afterthought in the draft, buried on the depth chart behind Drew Bledsoe.
However, these two men would go on to establish one of the most dominant dynasties in sports history through a combination of circumstance, preparation, and an unwavering pursuit of greatness. The Beginning – An Unlikely Trust Develops
Although Brady's rise in 2001 came as a surprise, Belichick quickly realized that he had a special quarterback in Brady. Belichick, who was known for being cold and critical, valued three qualities in a quarterback: The capacity to read defenses and make well-informed choices is called decision-making. A commitment to preparation and improvement is known as a work ethic. Mental toughness – The ability to handle pressure and adversity.
Brady excelled in all three areas.
When Drew Bledsoe suffered a life-threatening injury in Week 2 of the 2001 season, Belichick had a choice—stick with the experienced veteran or gamble on the unproven backup.
He chose Brady.
That decision changed NFL history.
Brady's Growth Under Belichick's System
Brady and Belichick were on the same page from the beginning. Belichick taught Brady how to dissect defenses, breaking down complex schemes and teaching him to anticipate coverages before the snap.

TOM BRADY BIOGRAPHY:

Brady embraced Belichick's insistence on perfection, diligently analyzing film and internalizing his coach's tactics. Both men were obsessed with winning and would give up everything else in order to compete for championships. Belichick was not known for his praise or sentimentality, so this partnership was not warm and emotional. But Brady didn't need encouragement. Belichick provided him with structure, discipline, and strategy when he needed it. A Superior Culture: The Patriotic Way The development of the Patriot Way, a team-first, no-excuses mentality that demanded excellence from everyone, was one of the Brady-Belichick era's hallmarks. No player was bigger than the team. It was expected of superstars to work as hard as rookies. Everything was prepared. Belichick drilled his players' minds with every possible scenario during lengthy film sessions. Errors were inexcusable. Regardless of their status, a player would be replaced if they failed to perform. Brady thrived in this environment.

Brady fully embraced Belichick's system, in contrast to many quarterbacks who desired the freedom to call their own plays and challenge their coaches. He studied more film than anyone.

He carried out the strategy without any ego. Even when coaching was harshly critical, he accepted it. Brady was the ideal quarterback for Belichick in many ways. The First Dynasty – Three Super Bowls in Four Years

Between 2001 and 2004, the Brady-Belichick duo dominated the NFL, winning three Super Bowls in four years.

Their formula was simple:

Elite preparation – No team outworked the Patriots.

Disciplined execution – Mistakes were minimized.

Situational mastery – The Patriots excelled in late-game situations.

Brady was the composed, decisive performer who thrived in pressure situations. Belichick was the cold, calculating mastermind who devised the perfect strategy.

They created the NFL's first genuine dynasty during the salary cap era. From Game Manager to GOAT: The Evolution As the years passed, Brady evolved, and so did his relationship with Belichick.

TOM BRADY BIOGRAPHY:

At first, people thought of him as a game manager—a quarterback who was good at running plays but wasn't expected to lead the offense. By the late 2000s, that perception changed.
Brady's football IQ had reached an elite level.
His arm strength and accuracy had improved.
He had mastered Belichick's complex offensive system.
Belichick, who is always willing to change, saw Brady's development and increased the offense. The result?
2007: Brady threw 50 touchdowns, leading the Patriots to an undefeated regular season.
2010s: The offense evolved into a high-powered passing attack, with Brady as the focal point.
Belichick no longer needed to supervise Brady because he could rely on him to direct the offense completely. This shift solidified Brady's status as the greatest quarterback of all time.
The Power Struggle – A Changing Dynamic
As Brady's greatness grew, so did the tension in his relationship with Belichick.
Brady had been treated by Belichick just like any other player for years: he gave him hard coaching, criticized him in meetings, and refused to treat him differently. But as Brady aged into his late 30s, things changed:
Brady desired increased involvement in personnel decisions. Belichick was reluctant to change his authoritarian style.
Brady's relationship with Robert Kraft, the owner of the team, grew stronger, raising the possibility of a divide. By 2017, the cracks in their partnership became visible:
According to reports, Belichick was dissatisfied with his decision to trade Jimmy Garoppolo, Brady's anticipated replacement. Brady's use of Alex Guerrero, his personal trainer, caused conflict with the team's medical staff. Some resentment resulted from Belichick's reluctance to give Brady preferential treatment. Despite the tension, they continued winning, adding three more Super Bowls to their resume.
The End of an Era – Brady Leaves New England
By 2019, it was clear that the Brady-Belichick partnership was nearing its end.

TOM BRADY BIOGRAPHY:

Even at 42, Brady still believed he could play at the highest level. But Belichick, always looking toward the future, seemed unwilling to commit to an aging quarterback.

Brady left New England in March 2020 to sign with the Tampa Bay Buccaneers, bringing an end to his career. The Brady-Belichick era was over for the first time in twenty years. Legacy of a Historic Partnership

Even after their split, their impact on the game remained undeniable. Together, they won six Super Bowls, more than any coach-quarterback duo in history.

They revolutionized the way teams approach game preparation and situational football.

Their success inspired a new generation of players and coaches.

However, this may have been their partnership's most defining feature: They weren't friends.

They were not required to be. They were two fierce, obsessive rivals who worked together to improve one another. Brady needed Belichick's structure and strategy to become the greatest quarterback of all time.

To establish the greatest dynasty in NFL history, Belichick required Brady's leadership and execution. Together, they created the most dominant era football has ever seen.

And no matter what came next, their legacy was etched in stone forever. Bill Belichick's tactical genius makes him the ideal coach for Brady. Their shared zeal for preparation and attention to detail was one of the main factors that contributed to the success of the Brady-Belichick partnership. Belichick was doing the same thing when it came to game planning and strategy, while Brady was meticulously conditioning his body and mind to become the best quarterback possible. Belichick had a reputation as one of the most innovative defensive minds in football. His ability to identify an opponent's weaknesses and exploit them was second to none. But he wasn't just a defensive mastermind—he was also a coach who understood the importance of adaptability.

He never committed to a single system or philosophy.

Every season, his team's identity changed based on the players. His coaching was based on what would give them the best chance to win that week.

TOM BRADY BIOGRAPHY:

Brady was the perfect quarterback for this system. He wasn't the most physically gifted or athletic quarterback, but he was a coach on the field who did exactly what Belichick needed in any game. Brady was a fan of structure despite the fact that many star quarterbacks demand offensive freedom. He trusted the process and saw the value in Belichick's game plans. This synergy is what made them unstoppable.

The Foundation of Trust: The First Super Bowl Victory If there was one moment that cemented the Brady-Belichick relationship, it was Super Bowl XXXVI against the St. Louis Rams.

The Rams had the most explosive offense in the league, known as "The Greatest Show on Turf."

They were 14-point favorites to win the game.

Most people thought New England wouldn't have a chance. But Belichick devised a masterful defensive game plan, one that would later be studied as one of the best in Super Bowl history.

His defense shut down the Rams' high-powered attack, holding them to just 17 points.

On offense, Brady executed a flawless game-winning drive, setting up Adam Vinatieri's iconic last-second field goal to secure the Patriots' first-ever Super Bowl title.

That victory wasn't just about winning a championship—it was about building belief.

Belichick's meticulous game planning gave them an advantage, as Brady witnessed firsthand. Belichick saw that Brady had the clutch gene, the ability to step up in the biggest moments.

It was the beginning of a dynasty.

The Patriot Way – The Power of a No-Nonsense Culture
If there was one thing that defined the Brady-Belichick era, it was the Patriot Way—a culture of accountability, discipline, and sacrifice.

Unlike other franchises that built their teams around superstar personalities, the Patriots focused on team-first mentality.

Belichick's philosophy was clear:

No one was bigger than the team.

Players were replaceable if they didn't buy into the system.

Only winning was important. Brady embodied this mindset perfectly.

TOM BRADY BIOGRAPHY:

He never complained about his contracts, often taking team-friendly deals to allow the Patriots to sign better players.

He wasn't obsessed with personal stats—all he cared about was winning championships.

He worked harder than anyone else, establishing a standard for all of the players in the locker room. Belichick, in turn, rewarded Brady by building the most fundamentally sound teams in football.

The Constant Evolution – How Brady and Belichick Adapted

The Patriots' capacity for change was one of the reasons why the dynasty lasted so long. Most NFL dynasties last four or five years before fading. The Brady-Belichick era lasted nearly two decades because they never became predictable.

Each stage of their dominance had a different identity:

Early 2000s (2001–2004): Defense-first, conservative offense.

Mid-2000s (2005–2009): Transitioning to an aggressive passing attack.

2010s: High-powered offenses built around Brady's quick decision-making.

Late 2010s: Balanced teams with a focus on efficiency.

Belichick constantly adjusted to new trends in the league, and Brady evolved his game accordingly.

Together, they proved that greatness isn't about sticking to one formula—it's about constantly finding new ways to win.

The Super Bowl Run in 2014 marked the turning point. While the Patriots had built one of the greatest dynasties in sports history, there was a 10-year gap between their third and fourth Super Bowl wins.

By 2014, critics began to wonder if Brady and Belichick were still the dominant team. That year, something changed.

Brady was as motivated as ever, feeding off the criticism.

Belichick made bold moves, including benching star cornerback Darrelle Revis in the playoffs.

The team had an edge, a hunger to prove they were still the best.

They were up against one of the greatest defenses of all time in Super Bowl XLIX against the Seattle Seahawks. It was Brady vs. the Legion of Boom.

After falling behind 24-14, Brady led two perfect fourth-quarter drives, throwing two clutch touchdowns to put New England ahead.

TOM BRADY BIOGRAPHY:

Then, in one of the most dramatic moments in Super Bowl history, Malcolm Butler's goal-line interception sealed the victory.
It was a defining moment—not just for the Patriots, but for Brady and Belichick's legacy.
The dynasty was reborn.
The Power Struggle – The Beginning of the End
As dominant as Brady and Belichick were together, friction was inevitable. By the late 2010s, cracks in their relationship started to show:
In 2014, Belichick selected Jimmy Garoppolo, indicating a possible strategy to succeed Brady. Following his own personal training regimen, Brady began working outside the Patriots' system. Brady's growing bond with Robert Kraft led to conflict with Belichick. The biggest sign of trouble came in 2018, when reports surfaced that Belichick wanted to keep Garoppolo, but Kraft sided with Brady, forcing a trade.
Brady felt disrespected because his coach continued to treat him as if he could be replaced after nearly two decades of dominance. Belichick felt frustrated—no player had ever been untouchable in his system.
The partnership, once unshakable, was starting to unravel.
One Last Victory Together at the Final Super Bowl The 2018 Super Bowl run was their final masterpiece together, despite the tension. Against the Los Angeles Rams in Super Bowl LIII, the Patriots delivered a defensive masterclass.
Brady wasn't at his best, but Belichick's defense dominated, holding the Rams to just 3 points—the lowest in Super Bowl history.
It was their sixth Super Bowl title together, tying the all-time record.
Fittingly, it was a game that showcased everything that made them great: Belichick's tactical genius.
Brady's leadership and poise.
The team-first mentality that had defined their dynasty.
The End – Brady Leaves New England
Even after the 2018 Super Bowl, the relationship between Brady and Belichick never fully recovered.
By 2019, it was clear that Belichick was looking to move on.
He refused to commit to Brady long-term.
He didn't surround him with top-tier offensive weapons.

TOM BRADY BIOGRAPHY:

He remained distant, treating Brady like just another player. In March 2020, Brady made the shocking decision to leave New England after 20 seasons.

The Brady-Belichick era had come to an end. Legacy of the Greatest Duo in Sports History

Even after their split, Brady and Belichick's impact on football is undeniable.

They won six Super Bowls together, the most in history.

They defined two decades of dominance.

They revolutionized the game, proving that success is built on preparation, discipline, and adaptability.

Brady and Belichick didn't need to be friends. They just needed to be the best football team ever. And they were.

TOM BRADY BIOGRAPHY:

CHAPTER NINE: THE GREATEST SUPER BOWL EVER: THE 28-3 COMEBACK

Super Bowl LI between the New England Patriots and the Atlanta Falcons on February 5, 2017, was more than just a championship game. As a demonstration of perseverance, strategy, and the will to win, it became a sporting moment that will never be forgotten. It was the turning point in Tom Brady's career. For Bill Belichick, it was another masterpiece of in-game coaching adjustments. Additionally, it served as a reminder of the perseverance of the Patriots as a group. But before the glory, there was disaster.

At one point in the third quarter, the Patriots were down 28-3. The Falcons had dominated every phase of the game, and the result seemed inevitable. No team had ever come back from a 25-point deficit in the Super Bowl.

However, Brady and the Patriots achieved the impossible in some way.

The Build-Up – Two Teams on a Collision Course

The Patriots entered Super Bowl LI as a battle-tested dynasty. They had already won four championships under Brady and Belichick, but their last Super Bowl victory had come two years earlier.

New England had endured a challenging season in 2016: The Deflategate scandal resulted in Brady's four-game suspension. They had to rely on backup quarterbacks for a portion of the season.

Since their previous Super Bowl run, the roster had undergone significant changes. Despite all of this, the Patriots still finished 14-2, with Brady playing some of the best football of his career. At age 39, he had thrown 28 touchdowns and just 2 interceptions, leading New England to yet another AFC Championship.

On the other side, the Atlanta Falcons were a team on the rise. Led by quarterback Matt Ryan and offensive coordinator Kyle Shanahan, the Falcons boasted the NFL's highest-scoring offense.

After throwing for 4,944 yards and 38 touchdowns, Ryan won MVP. Wide receiver Julio Jones was a nightmare for defenses.

The running back duo of Devonta Freeman and Tevin Coleman gave them balance.

TOM BRADY BIOGRAPHY:

Their offense had shredded teams all season, and they had just dismantled the Green Bay Packers in the NFC Championship.
Heading into the Super Bowl, the question was: Could the Patriots stop Atlanta's offensive juggernaut?
New England's nightmare in the first half Both defenses played well at the beginning of the game. Neither team scored in the first quarter, but Atlanta struck first in the second quarter—and the floodgates opened.
Devonta Freeman broke loose for a 5-yard touchdown run, putting the Falcons up 7-0.
On the next drive, Matt Ryan surgically picked apart the Patriots defense, leading to a 19-yard touchdown pass to Austin Hooper.
When Brady threw a rare interception, Atlanta's defense capitalized—Robert Alford returned it 82 yards for a touchdown.
Suddenly, it was 21-0, and the Patriots were in serious trouble.
They managed to get on the board before halftime with a field goal, but the scoreboard still read Falcons 21, Patriots 3 at the break.
Brady's mindset and Belichick's adjustments at halftime As the Patriots entered the locker room, the mood was tense.
In a Super Bowl, no team had ever overcome a deficit of more than 10 points. They had been outplayed by the Falcons at every stage of the game. Brady had been repeatedly hit by Atlanta's defense, which had been relentless. The combination of Belichick and Brady made all the difference in this situation. Belichick, always cold and calculated, began dissecting what was going wrong.
He adjusted the defensive scheme, switching to more aggressive coverage on Julio Jones.
He shifted the offensive strategy, telling Brady to concentrate on quick, short passes rather than deep shots. Brady, on the other hand, was totally focused. He gathered his teammates and delivered a simple message: "We just need one drive. One play at a time."
He had been here before, so the scoreboard didn't bother him. He knew if they could score once, momentum could shift.
The Third Quarter – The Hole Gets Deeper
Whatever adjustments the Patriots had made at halftime didn't seem to matter at first.

TOM BRADY BIOGRAPHY:

Early in the third quarter, Atlanta extended their lead.
Ryan found Tevin Coleman for a 6-yard touchdown pass, making it 28-3.
The Falcons sideline erupted.
The Patriots appeared to be defeated. That would have been the end for most teams. But this was Brady. This was Belichick.
The Turning Point – A Small Spark
With two minutes left in the third quarter, the Patriots finally found the end zone.
During a fast-paced drive, Brady distributed the ball to multiple receivers. Running back James White punched it in for a 5-yard touchdown run.
The Patriots lined up for the extra point—but it was blocked.
It remained 28-9. The mountain was immense, but they had finally scored.
The Fourth Quarter – The Greatest Comeback Begins
Legends are made during Super Bowl LI's fourth quarter. The Patriots needed three touchdowns and two two-point conversions just to tie the game.
The majority of teams never even considered it. But Brady was relentless.
1. First Scoring Drive – 28-12
The Patriots forced a Falcons punt.
Brady used quick throws to attack the middle of the field. Stephen Gostkowski hit a field goal to make it 28-12.
2. The Defense Steps Up
Atlanta got the ball back, needing only a few first downs to put the game away.
Matt Ryan was sacked by the Patriots, who recovered the fumble. 3. Second Scoring Drive – 28-20
Brady found Danny Amendola for a touchdown.
James White converted the two-point attempt.
Suddenly, it was 28-20 with six minutes left.
4. Julio Jones' Catch – A Near-Death Blow
Matt Ryan responded with a miracle sideline catch by Julio Jones.
Atlanta was already in field goal range, where three points would end the game.
5. The Sack That Saved the Patriots

TOM BRADY BIOGRAPHY:

Ryan was sacked once more by the Patriots, putting them out of range for a field goal. The Falcons were forced to punt.

6. Final Drive – The Greatest Play in Super Bowl History

Brady led a 91-yard drive in two minutes.

Julian Edelman made an impossible catch, keeping the drive alive.

With less than a minute remaining, James White scored. 7. Two-Point Conversion – 28-28

The Patriots needed one last play to tie the game.

Amendola was hit by Brady for the two-point conversion. Super Bowl LI was going to overtime.

Overtime – Sealing the Comeback

The Patriots never looked back after winning the coin toss. Brady made five consecutive passes as he carefully drove the team down the field. At the 2-yard line, James White powered through the defense for the game-winning touchdown.

Final Score: New England 34, Atlanta 28. The greatest Super Bowl comeback was completed. Brady had thrown 466 yards, earning his fifth Super Bowl title and proving, beyond any doubt, that he was the greatest quarterback of all time.

Disbelief and the Making of History in the Aftermath The Patriots' sideline burst into cheers as James White crossed the goal line in overtime to complete the greatest comeback in Super Bowl history. Tom Brady collapsed to the ground and let out a mixture of exhaustion and joy as he was emotionally overburdened. The scoreboard at NRG Stadium in Houston, Texas, read New England 34, Atlanta 28—a result that, just an hour earlier, seemed impossible.

The entire football world was in shock.

The spectators couldn't believe what they had seen. The Patriots had trailed by 25 points—a deficit no team had ever overcome in a Super Bowl.

The Falcons were taken aback as their championship hopes were brutally dashed. Sports analysts scrambled to put the comeback into perspective, many declaring it the greatest moment in NFL history.

For the fourth time in his career, Brady won the Super Bowl MVP award after throwing for 466 yards, the most in Super Bowl history at the time. His fifth Super Bowl victory made him the most successful quarterback in the

TOM BRADY BIOGRAPHY:

game's history, surpassing Joe Montana and Terry Bradshaw. After the game, even Brady admitted that he never considered the odds. He just knew he had to keep fighting.

A Cementation of a Legacy at the Patriots' Celebration As the Lombardi Trophy was brought onto the stage, Patriots owner Robert Kraft took the microphone.

He called the victory "unequivocally the sweetest," a clear shot at Deflategate, which had overshadowed the Patriots in the previous two seasons.

For Brady, this moment was deeply personal. He was holding the trophy in the same season he had been suspended for four games. Many had doubted whether he could still win at the highest level, but he had silenced every critic in the most spectacular way possible.

His mother, Galynn Brady, who had been battling cancer and had barely attended any games that season, was present in the stadium. For Brady, winning this title with her watching made it even more meaningful.

The Falcons' Collapse – A Devastating Loss

The Atlanta Falcons, on the other hand, were in shock. At halftime, they had been so close to victory that they could almost touch the trophy.

With just 8:31 left in the game, they still led 28-12.

At 4:40 left, they were in field goal range—one kick would have put the game out of reach.

And yet, they let it slip away.

This loss haunted the Falcons for years.

Head coach Dan Quinn was heavily criticized for his game management.

Offensive coordinator Kyle Shanahan, who had called aggressive plays instead of running out the clock, was blamed for not being conservative enough.

Matt Ryan, the league MVP, played an incredible game but would forever be associated with blowing a 28-3 lead.

Even years later, whenever the number 28-3 was mentioned, it became a painful reminder of what could have been.

The X-Factors Behind the Comeback – How the Patriots Did It

TOM BRADY BIOGRAPHY:

New England's comeback wasn't just about Brady's brilliance—it was a combination of several key factors that all came together in the perfect storm.

1. The relentless conditioning of the Patriots The Patriots were known for having one of the best-conditioned teams in the NFL.

Belichick ran grueling practices.

The team emphasized stamina and endurance more than most.

By the fourth quarter, when most teams were exhausted, the Patriots still had energy left.

New England continued to play at full speed even as the Falcons' defense began to tire. 2. Belichick's Second-Half Adjustments

Belichick is famous for his in-game coaching adjustments, and this game was a masterclass in how to change strategy mid-game.

The Patriots' defense had a hard time stopping Atlanta in the first half. At halftime, Belichick shifted coverages, putting extra defenders on Julio Jones and focusing on stopping the run.

The Patriots' defensive line attacked Matt Ryan more aggressively, forcing sacks and a critical fumble.

His ability to adapt on the fly was one of the biggest reasons for the comeback.

3. James White – The Unsung Hero

While Brady was the face of the comeback, running back James White had one of the greatest performances in Super Bowl history.

He had 14 receptions for 110 yards—a Super Bowl record for a running back.

He finished with three touchdowns, including the one that won the game. His two-point conversion late in the fourth quarter was a must-have play.

Brady later said White should have been Super Bowl MVP.

4. The Julian Edelman Catch – The Miracle Play

Every great comeback has a miracle play, and in this game, it was Julian Edelman's impossible catch.

With the Patriots trailing 28-20, Brady fired a pass over the middle that was deflected by a Falcons defender.

The ball bounced in the air.

TOM BRADY BIOGRAPHY:

Edelman dove forward, reached out, and somehow snatched it inches from the ground.

He held on despite being surrounded by three Falcons players. The play was reviewed and confirmed as a catch, keeping the drive alive.

The Legacy of Super Bowl LI

The greatest comeback in NFL history still holds true years after this game. Tom Brady's legacy was forever changed. He was no longer just the most accomplished quarterback—he was now the greatest of all time.

Bill Belichick proved once again that no coach could outthink him when it mattered most.

The Patriots established their dynasty as the most resilient team in NFL history.

For the Falcons, the loss became a curse.

They never fully recovered from 28-3.

Kyle Shanahan left Atlanta to coach the 49ers.

Matt Ryan never returned to a Super Bowl.

Brady's Personal Reflection – A Victory for the Ages

Years later, Brady called Super Bowl LI "the most satisfying win of my career."

Not just because of the comeback, but because of everything that led up to it—the Deflategate suspension, the doubts about his age, and the years of preparation.

It was a game of perseverance.

A reminder to never quit, no matter the circumstances.

More than just a Super Bowl, this game was a turning point in sports history. And at the center of it all was Tom Brady, proving once and for all that he was the greatest to ever play the game.

TOM BRADY BIOGRAPHY:

CHAPTER TEN: LESSONS FROM TOM BRADY – WHAT WE CAN LEARN FROM HIS JOURNEY

Tom Brady's career is more than just a story of football dominance. His journey from an overlooked draft pick to the greatest quarterback of all time holds lessons for athletes, professionals, and anyone striving for greatness. His success was never just about talent—it was built on discipline, work ethic, leadership, and an unshakable belief in himself.

Brady's story teaches us how to handle setbacks, how to outwork competitors, and how to remain focused on long-term success. Every step of his career—from his struggles in college, being the 199th pick in the draft, his first Super Bowl, the 28-3 comeback, and even his late-career success with the Tampa Bay Buccaneers—provides insight into what it takes to be the best.

Any field, including sports, business, or personal development, can benefit from his mindset, preparedness, resilience, and leadership skills. Lesson 1: The Power of Self-Belief – Betting on Yourself

Tom Brady did not possess the greatest physical ability. He didn't have a rocket arm like Brett Favre.

He was not as mobile as Lamar Jackson or Michael Vick. He wasn't a highly touted draft prospect like Peyton Manning.

Yet, he always believed in himself.

When he arrived at the University of Michigan and was buried on the depth chart, he didn't let it shake his confidence.

He was still confident that he would be a starter in the NFL when he was selected 199th overall. He told Robert Kraft, "I'm the best decision this franchise has ever made," when he was benched in favor of Drew Bledsoe early in his career. Many people let opinions from other people define them. Brady never did.

He had an unshakable internal belief in his ability, which gave him the resilience to keep improving. This mindset applies to any field—whether you're a young professional trying to prove yourself or an entrepreneur launching a business.

Lesson 2: Outwork Everyone – The Obsession with Improvement

Brady's work ethic is legendary.

TOM BRADY BIOGRAPHY:

He studied film for longer than any other quarterback. He treated each repetition in practice like it was the Super Bowl. His offseason training was so intense and detailed that his body remained elite well into his 40s.
Many quarterbacks rely on natural talent. Brady relied on preparation and hard work.
He was the first player in the facility at 5 AM and often the last to leave.
He was more familiar with his foes than they were with themselves and diligently studied their defenses. In the offseason, he trained, recovered, and prepared for the upcoming season. He did not party. What does this mean? Talent alone is not enough to achieve success; one must also put in the time. In any field, people who are always looking for ways to improve will stand out from those who are just doing what needs to be done. Lesson 3: Resilience in the Face of Obstacles Brady's career was fraught with failures: At Michigan, he was a backup for two years before earning the starting job.
He was drafted in the sixth round and nearly went undrafted.
He lost three Super Bowls, the best of which was in 2007. He suffered a devastating ACL injury in 2008, missing the entire season.
Deflategate resulted in a four-game suspension for him in 2016. But he never made excuses.
Instead, he used setbacks as fuel.
He returned after a perfect season and won three more Super Bowls. He extended his career and revised his training schedule following his injury. He led the Patriots to a Super Bowl comeback victory over Atlanta following his suspension. Brady teaches us that failure is not the end; rather, it is just one more step on the way. Life will always throw challenges our way. How we react is what matters. The fourth lesson in leadership is about raising others up. Great leaders don't just succeed themselves—they make everyone around them better.
Brady wasn't just a great player; he was a great leader.
He set the tone in the locker room.
He never blamed teammates for mistakes—he took responsibility.
He demanded excellence without arrogance.

TOM BRADY BIOGRAPHY:

When Brady joined the Tampa Bay Buccaneers in 2020, the team hadn't made the playoffs in 13 years. One year later, they were Super Bowl champions.

Why? Because Brady changed the culture.

He persuaded teammates to work out harder. From superstars to backups, he developed relationships with every player. He made everyone believe they could win.

Leadership isn't about a title—it's about influencing and elevating those around you.

Lesson 5: The Value of Routine and Consistency Brady's success was not based on a single pivotal moment. It was built on decades of consistent habits. He followed the TB12 Method, a disciplined approach to health and recovery.

He had the same routine every day—waking up, eating right, training, studying film.

He treated every practice, offseason, and meeting as if it were critical.

Success in any field is about repeating great habits every single day.

If you want to be fit, you don't go to the gym once—you work out consistently.

If you want to be a great writer, entrepreneur, or musician, you don't have to rely on inspiration; rather, you have to develop habits that help you keep getting better. Brady's success was based on the small things he did every day. Lesson 6: Staying Hungry – Never Being Satisfied

Even after winning seven Super Bowls, Brady never became complacent. After winning a championship, he immediately started planning for the next season.

He always acted as though he had something to prove and never felt like he had "arrived." Even when he had completed everything, he was still hungry. Most people stop pushing when they reach a certain level of success. Brady never did. He always found new challenges—whether it was proving he could win after Deflategate, proving he could win after leaving New England, or proving he could still play at age 44.

The lesson? Never give up. Success is a lifelong journey, not a destination. One of Tom Brady's greatest strengths was his ability to

TOM BRADY BIOGRAPHY:

perform under immense pressure. Some athletes and professionals crumble in high-stakes moments. Brady thrived.

Super Bowl XXXVI (2001): In just his first season as a starter, Brady led the Patriots on a game-winning drive in the Super Bowl against the Rams, despite being just 24 years old.

Super Bowl XLIX (2014): Down 10 points in the fourth quarter against the Seahawks, he led two touchdown drives to win his fourth Super Bowl.

Super Bowl LI (2016): The most famous example—he erased a 28-3 deficit to complete the greatest comeback in NFL history.

The secret? Composure, focus, and an unshakable belief in himself.

Brady didn't let fear or anxiety take over. He had a short memory for failure—when he made a mistake, he immediately moved on.

The takeaway from this is clear: Pressure is a privilege. It indicates that you can achieve success. Preparation leads to confidence. Brady prepared so intensely that when the biggest moments came, he had no reason to panic.

Never let emotions cloud your judgment. Instead of overreacting, trust your training and execute.

Whether in sports, business, or personal challenges, mental toughness separates the good from the great.

Lesson 8: Adapting and Evolving – Longevity in a Competitive World

Brady's career lasted over two decades, a feat almost unheard of in professional football. How did he do it? By constantly evolving.

Early in his career, he relied on quick, short throws and a defensive-minded team.

In the 2007 season, he transformed into a deep-ball passer with Randy Moss.

In his 40s, he adjusted his game to focus on pre-snap reads and faster decision-making.

In Tampa Bay, he learned a new offensive system, proving he could win outside of New England.

The ability to adapt is crucial in any career.

Companies that don't change, like Blockbuster and Kodak, fall behind. People who hold on to skills that are no longer relevant are replaced. Those who embrace change—like Brady—stay at the top for years.

TOM BRADY BIOGRAPHY:

The lesson? Keep learning, keep adjusting, and stay ahead of the competition.

Lesson 9: Sacrifice – The Price of Greatness

Brady's career wasn't just about hard work—it was about sacrifice.

He sacrificed social life and distractions to stay fully committed to football.

He signed contracts favorable to the team so that the Patriots could afford better players. To keep performing at his best, he ate a lot and worked out a lot. Many people want success, but few are willing to make the sacrifices necessary to achieve it.

While others are out partying, great musicians spend hours practicing. Successful entrepreneurs work early mornings and late nights to build something great.

Elite athletes like Brady eliminate distractions and fully commit to their craft.

The takeaway? Success requires sacrifice. The question is: How much are you willing to give up to achieve greatness?

Lesson 10: Never Let Others Define Your Limits

People undervalued Brady from the moment he joined the NFL. Scouts said he was too slow and had a weak arm.

Coaches initially doubted whether he could even be a backup.

He was criticized as a "system quarterback" who would not succeed without Belichick, according to critics. Time and time again, he proved them all wrong.

The point? Don't let what other people think about you become your reality. If you're an artist and people say you'll never make it, prove them wrong by improving your craft.

If you're in a job where no one sees your potential, outwork everyone and make them notice.

If someone says your goals are too big, let that fuel your determination instead of discouraging you.

Brady's mindset was simple: The only person who decides what you can or can't do is you.

Lesson 11: The Importance of Passion – Love What You Do

Brady didn't just play football for money or fame—he genuinely loved the game.

TOM BRADY BIOGRAPHY:

Even in his 40s, he was still excited about practice. He studied film with the enthusiasm of a rookie.

Even after winning seven Super Bowls, he still had the hunger to compete.

Many people chase careers for status or financial rewards, but true greatness comes from passion.

If you truly love what you do, then:

You'll work harder than anyone else.

You won't burn out, because your work energizes you.

You'll keep improving, even after success.

The lesson? Find something you're passionate about and give it all of your attention. Lesson 12: Make sure the right people surround you. Brady's success wasn't just about his own work—it was also about the team and mentors around him.

He had Bill Belichick, one of the greatest coaches in history, who pushed him to be better.

He trained with Alex Guerrero, who helped him maintain peak physical health for decades.

He surrounded himself with teammates who shared his championship mindset.

Who you surround yourself with matters.

If you're around negative people, they will hold you back.

If you spend time with driven, ambitious individuals, they will push you to new heights.

Brady always sought out people who could help him grow, and that played a huge role in his longevity and success.

Lesson 13: Never Be Afraid to Take Risks

When Brady left New England after 20 years, many people wondered if he could succeed elsewhere. He was 43 years old and joining a new team, new coach, and new city.

Many athletes in his position would have retired to protect their legacy. But Brady took the risk—and won another Super Bowl.

The lesson? Sometimes, taking a big risk is necessary for growth.

Whether it's changing careers, starting a business, or moving to a new place, staying comfortable doesn't lead to breakthroughs.

TOM BRADY BIOGRAPHY:

Instead, Brady demonstrated that he is capable of winning in any situation, so he could have continued his career in New England. Success often requires stepping outside your comfort zone.

Lesson 14: The Legacy of Excellence – Leave a Mark

At the end of the day, Brady's career wasn't just about his numbers or rings—it was about how he inspired millions of people.

He showed that hard work beats talent when talent doesn't work hard.

He proved that age is just a number if you take care of yourself.

He encouraged dreamers, athletes, and business leaders to go above and beyond. The true measure of greatness isn't just what you achieve—it's how many people you inspire along the way.

Final Takeaway – Apply Brady's Lessons to Your Own Life

Tom Brady's journey isn't just about football—it's about what's possible when you fully commit to a goal.

Whether you're an athlete, entrepreneur, artist, or student, these lessons apply:

1. Believe in yourself, even when no one else does.
2. Outwork everyone.
3. Use setbacks as fuel.
4. Lead by example.
5. Stay consistent and disciplined.
6. Never be satisfied—keep growing.
7. Embrace challenges and pressure.
8. Be surrounded by the right people.
9. Step outside of your comfort zone and take risks.
10. Leave behind a legacy of excellence.

Brady's story shows us that greatness isn't about luck—it's about commitment, preparation, and the relentless pursuit of excellence.

TOM BRADY BIOGRAPHY:

CONCLUSION

The End: A Legacy Long Past the Game The story of Tom Brady goes beyond football dominance. It is the pinnacle example of the power of perseverance, a strong work ethic, and the unwavering pursuit of excellence. His career reshaped the boundaries of what is possible in professional sports, taking him from a draft pick in the sixth round with low expectations to the undisputed best quarterback in NFL history. Brady did not possess the strongest arm, the fastest legs, or the most imposing physique. What he had was something far greater—an obsessive commitment to preparation, a deep understanding of the game, and an unyielding competitive fire that burned brighter with every passing year. His career was a great example of how to overcome doubt, silence critics, and demonstrate that greatness is earned rather than acquired. Against All Odds, Time and Time Again From the moment he entered the NFL, Brady faced obstacles. He began as the fourth-string quarterback for the New England Patriots, buried on the depth chart behind Drew Bledsoe and other more highly regarded prospects. Few saw him as the future of the franchise. Brady was seen as a short-term replacement rather than a long-term solution even when Bledsoe died in 2001. Yet, week after week, game after game, season after season, Brady shattered expectations. He led the Patriots to a Super Bowl victory in his first full season as a starter, then built a dynasty that would define an entire era of football. With every comeback, every improbable win, and every championship, Brady reinforced the idea that the only limits are the ones others place on you.
 He was repeatedly ruled out. After a decade-long Super Bowl drought between 2005 and 2014, people questioned whether his best days were behind him. Critics speculated that he would not succeed without Bill Belichick's system when he left the Patriots in 2020. And yet, time after time, Brady responded the only way he knew how—by winning. His seventh and final Super Bowl, won with the Tampa Bay Buccaneers at the age of 43, was the ultimate proof that greatness follows those who refuse to accept limitations.
 A Blueprint for Success Beyond Football

TOM BRADY BIOGRAPHY:

Brady's impact extends far beyond the football field. His meticulous approach to training, his dedication to longevity, and his leadership have set new standards for athletes across all sports. His TB12 Method, which was once thought to be unconventional, is now widely studied as a blueprint for performance and recovery. He did more than just succeed; he also rethought the criteria for success. Beyond that, the lessons that Brady's leadership, ability to motivate those around him, and unwavering belief in his own capabilities impart transcend sports are lessons. His career teaches us that:

Hard work beats talent when talent doesn't work hard.

Every setback is an opportunity to rise again.

Success is built in the unseen hours, in preparation, discipline, and relentless improvement.

The greatest battles are won in the mind long before they are won on the field.

The Lasting Legacy of Tom Brady

When the final chapter of his playing career was written, Tom Brady stood atop the NFL with seven Super Bowl titles, five Super Bowl MVPs, three league MVPs, and nearly every major passing record. But his legacy is not just in the numbers. His legacy is in the moments—the improbable comebacks, the iconic throws, the cold-blooded performances under pressure.

He didn't just win. He dominated for over two decades in a sport designed to humble even the best. He outlasted generations of challengers, adapted to changing eras, and remained at the pinnacle of football longer than anyone thought possible.

For those who watched his career unfold, Tom Brady was more than just a quarterback. He was an example of what can be accomplished with unshakable belief, relentless preparation, and an unwillingness to accept anything less than greatness.

From 199th Pick to Immortal Legend

Tom Brady's journey is the greatest underdog story in sports history. He entered the NFL as an afterthought. He regarded it as his best performance ever. His story serves as a reminder that greatness is not given—it is earned through years of sacrifice, discipline, and an unrelenting

TOM BRADY BIOGRAPHY:

pursuit of being the best. It is a lesson to every overlooked athlete, every underestimated competitor, and every person striving to achieve something greater than themselves.

Brady was not supposed to be the best. But in the end, he became the greatest of all time.

And for that, his legacy will live forever.

Made in United States
North Haven, CT
22 July 2025